ZOMBIES

Not so long ago zombies rarely shuffled out of B-grade horror movies and cult comic books, but today they are everywhere. Zombies are proliferating, demonstrating an extraordinary capacity to transport fluidly from genre to genre, from the apocalyptic future to the already survived past, and in and out of fictional form.

Today they can be found in just about any genre or discourse and as they move sinuously across the cultural landscape they keep morphing; taking on ever new and ever more bizarre associations. Zombies would appear to be unthinkable, the ultimate nightmare of a world devoured by the dead, and yet more and more often this horror-scape provides a form of figurative capture for the way things are. This book explores why.

Zombies explores the recent transformation of zombie from cult genre to a figure that pervades western culture. Rutherford examines the zombie as a powerful metaphor for a constellation of social forces that define contemporary reality. This is an ideal introduction to all that is social about zombies, for students and general readers alike.

Jennifer Rutherford is a sociologist and literary scholar, and is currently Deputy Director of the Hawke Research Institute at the University of South Australia.

SHORTCUTS – *Little Books on Big Issues'*

Shortcuts is a major new series of concise, accessible introductions to some of the major issues of our times. The series is developed as an A to Z coverage of emergent or new social, cultural and political phenomenon. Issues and topics covered range from food to fat, from climate change to suicide bombing, from love to zombies. Whilst the principal focus of **Shortcuts** is the relevance of current issues, topics and debates to the social sciences and humanities, the books should also appeal to a wider audience seeking guidance on how to engage with today's leading social, political and philosophical debates.

Series Editor: Anthony Elliott is Director of the Hawke Research Institute, where he is Research Professor of Sociology at the University of South Australia.

Titles in the series:

Confronting Climate Change
Constance Lever-Tracy

Feelings
Stephen Frosh

Suicide Bombings
Riaz Hassan

Web 2.0
Sam Han

Global Finance
Robert J. Holton

Freedom
Nick Stevenson

Planet Sport
Kath Woodward

Fat
Deborah Lupton

Reinvention
Anthony Elliott

Panic
Keith Tester

Love
Tom Inglis

Food
John Coveney

Zombies
Jennifer Rutherford

ZOMBIES

Jennifer Rutherford

Routledge
Taylor & Francis Group
LONDON AND NEW YORK

First published 2013
by Routledge
2 Park Square, Milton Park, Abingdon, Oxon OX14 4RN

and by Routledge
711 Third Avenue, New York, NY 10017

Routledge is an imprint of the Taylor & Francis Group, an informa business

© 2013 Jennifer Rutherford

The right of Jennifer Rutherford to be identified as author of this work has been asserted by her in accordance with sections 77 and 78 of the Copyright, Designs and Patents Act 1988.

All rights reserved. No part of this book may be reprinted or reproduced or utilised in any form or by any electronic, mechanical, or other means, now known or hereafter invented, including photocopying and recording, or in any information storage or retrieval system, without permission in writing from the publishers.

Trademark notice: Product or corporate names may be trademarks or registered trademarks, and are used only for identification and explanation without intent to infringe.

British Library Cataloguing in Publication Data
A catalogue record for this book is available from the British Library

Library of Congress Cataloging in Publication Data
Rutherford, Jennifer.
Zombies / Jennifer Rutherford.
pages cm. – (Shortcuts)
1. Zombies. I. Title.
GR581.R87 2013
398'.45–dc23
2013008458

ISBN: 978-0-415-52447-6 (hbk)
ISBN: 978-0-415-52448-3 (pbk)
ISBN: 978-0-203-10184-1 (ebk)

Typeset in Bembo by Cenveo Publisher Services

Printed and bound in the United States of America by Edwards Brothers Malloy

For Phoebe and Benedicte

CONTENTS

List of figures	*x*
Series Editor's preface	*xi*
Acknowledgements	*xiii*
1 Monstration	1
2 The collective zombie	25
3 Zombie erotics	48
4 The zombie opera	61
5 Carrion dreams	84
Notes	*99*
Bibliography	*101*
Index	*109*

LIST OF FIGURES

0.1	Street graffiti	xiv
1.1	Zombie wedding, zombie parade, Adelaide, October 2012	4
3.1	Family feast, zombie parade, Adelaide, October 2012	55
4.1	Zombie marines, zombie parade, Adelaide, October 2012	83

SHORTCUTS – 'Little Books on Big Issues'

Series Editor's preface

Shortcuts is a major new series of concise, accessible introductions to some of the major issues of our times. The series is developed as an A to Z coverage of emergent or new social, cultural and political phenomena. Issues and topics covered range from food to fat, from climate change to suicide bombing, from love to zombies. Whilst the principal focus of *Shortcuts* is the relevance of current issues, topics and debates to the social sciences and humanities, the books should also appeal to a wider audience seeking guidance on how to engage with today's leading social, political and philosophical debates.

The rise of zombie-related popular culture and associated social anxieties about the living dead speaks volumes about an era shaped to its roots by a global war on terror. Yet on the whole the social sciences, despite their fascination with monstrous, infected Others, have had little to say on zombies. In this brilliant book, Jennifer Rutherford considers zombies – those 'gate-crashing creatures' – anew, as figures at once emptying meaning whilst also proliferating it. Perhaps the contemporary hook of zombies arises because we postmoderns – cool, laid-back, fractured and decentred – lack the depth that reflective, autonomous subjectivity requires. Rutherford speculates on this, and a great deal more besides. From zombie horror films to zombie porn, and from *Night of the Living Dead* to *The Walking Dead*, Rutherford sees in zombie culture a metatrope which has metastasised! Rutherford's *Zombies* truly dazzles.

Anthony Elliott

ACKNOWLEDGEMENTS

I am grateful for the help of friends and colleagues. In particular, Barbara Holloway for her careful proofing and insightful comments on the manuscript, and Rita Horanyi for her help with research assistance, formatting and preparing the manuscript and bibliography. Kathleen Fallon provided many zombie references (especially Leah Gordon's extraordinary photographs of Kanaval in Haiti) and also much support along the way. I'd also like to thank Daniel Chaffee and Tamara Waraschinki for their discussions and helpful references and in particular Ann McCulloch and the organisers and participants at the Double Dialogues conference at the University of the South Pacific in 2012, where some of these ideas were first trialled; Anthony Elliott for many discussions and for originally suggesting the book. Flinders University School of Social and Policy Studies provided a grant that enabled me to undertake research for this project. Thanks also for the professional input, assistance and support from Routledge, especially Gerhard Boomgaardern, Emily Briggs, Peter Lloyd and Chris Shaw, the copy editor. I'd also like to thank Kate Leeson. Some excerpts in Chapter 5 were originally published in Rutherford, J. (ed.) (1997) 'Diana: the hour of our death', in Ien Ang (ed.) *Planet Diana: Cultural Studies and Global Mourning*, Kingswood, NSW: University of Western Sydney Press. Finally I would especially like to thank my family, Brian, Phoebe and Bene, who suffered a long summer given over to zombies.

Si vis vitam, para mortem.
If you wish life, prepare for death.

— Sigmund Freud

FIGURE 0.1 Street graffiti.

1
MONSTRATION

One day, I was walking down one of the wide tree-lined streets of Adelaide, the provincial city where I live in Australia, when I spied some graffiti. These two armed figures calling for 'Brains' were surprising. They brought to mind the graffiti art of the sixties and seventies known as the radical stencil movement, that began with the student-led revolution in France in 1968. Quick, cheap, mobile and easily reproducible, stencils were a perfect medium for plastering the streets with revolutionary pictograms and slogans. They often had a violent tinge to them, like the endlessly repeated image of one man holding a pistol to the head of another, underwritten by the word 'Capitalism'. Zombie manifestations often draw on the mantras and icons of left-wing causes of the past – like the zombie chant: 'What do we want? Brains! When do we want them? Now!' Could this zombie graffiti have a revolutionary ancestry? If so, I had to wonder what the underlying idea or cause at work was here. I also wondered if this was the work of a sole zombie-obsessed graffitist plastering the city's telegraph poles with the zombie mantra: 'BRAINS', or was the ever-spreading zombie obsession building its own sub-culture in the churchy and rather elegant city of Adelaide?

My first answer to these questions came some time later at the annual zombie parade. Adelaide prides itself on not having started life as a penal colony and it also boasts a less bloodspattered colonial past than the rest of Australia, which some say explains its pronounced gentility. Surprise then to find Adelaidean zombies in the street in their thousands. This was no small zombie parade but a *monstration* equal to any of the zombie festivals being held in far more troubled cities across the world. Adelaide might not be Atlanta, Seattle or Pittsburgh (Brown, 2011) – cities fighting it out to claim the title of 'zombie capital of the world' – but here, as elsewhere, zombies were on the move.

It's easy to assume that zombies find their following amongst the young and frivolous. Not so. Zombies are a dead menace when it comes to breaking down all kinds of barriers. On the screen they've shown a complete disregard for generic boundaries and at the Adelaide zombie parade they were showing scant regard for demographic boundaries. They were young and old, straight and queer, alone, in groups and *en famille*. As I walked through the crowds it was clear that here were people from both the Southern 'burbs' and the *beau quartier*. A few possessed an art school cool; others were proudly 'bogan'.[1] Some quaffed blood from champagne flutes; others chewed on bones as they chugged down a 'tinny'.[2]

Zombies are the *parvenus* of the undead lacking the long ancestry of their vampire cousins – the modern Zombie only really takes form in Romero's first film *Night of the Living Dead* (1968) – but these latter-day creatures were claiming a literary lineage that stretched back for centuries. Alongside the familiar shuffling figures of zombie notoriety – zombie doctors and nurses, zombie brides and their blood-spattered grooms, teddy-bear clutching zombie kids and their hungry mums, all the everyman and everywoman zombies of everyday life – there were Zombies cast from the entire character repertoire of text and screen. Bonneted and blood smeared, Elizabeth Bennet chewed wantonly on Mr Darcy's edible bits. Zombie Snow-White and zombie Bo-Peep picnicked alongside Zombie hobbits and Hogwartians. Zombie soldiers of every epoch shared blood with their more familiar prototypes – zombie Nazis and zombie marines. A zombie Christ sprinkled blessings on a Japanese zombie flower girl who could have been one of those ravaged wanderers in the aftermath of Hiroshima. And, most strange of all, real life mums and dads paraded their real life kids as zombie offspring in gore-splattered cowboy suits and fairy dresses. These people were not just playing dress-ups with the walking dead, they were playing dress-ups with history, morphing the literal and literary past through the lens of the zombie fantasy as if to prove that everything – past, present and future – could be zombified. Given that the zombie narrative is all about an apocalyptic future, this reaching back into the past was a bit of a puzzle. I decided to put it on my list of bewildering things that need to be understood about zombies today. This list – beginning with the question, 'What is a zombie?' – has been proliferating for some time.

Bewilderment

When I first started watching zombie films about a decade ago, it was during a time in my life – I would have to say a very bad time in my life – when being hurled into the chaotic and violent world of a zombie film made me feel, frankly, at home. My own world had crumpled suddenly and I was surviving – just. Someone, *the One*, was acting like a zombie, and keeping myself and my children afloat in this strange new world of torn meanings felt like surviving a zombie apocalypse. Back then, *The Zombie Survival Guide* (Brooks, 2003) had not yet been written, so I made do with watching movies. Night after night, I would nurse myself to sleep with the comfort found in the dark, decombusting world of zombie.

In every zombie fiction (post-1968) there's a moment, I call it the zombie moment, when a choice is offered to the protagonist: smash in the head of your husband, mother, sister, brother, child, or lover, or join them in a zombie embrace. It's a situation all too familiar to anyone who's been through a nasty divorce. Love in the universe of zombie is, to borrow Zygmunt Bauman's (2003) term, in a 'liquid' state.[3] No bond can endure a bite and the price of nostalgia is evisceration. Characters in zombie fictions have to respond to this changed emotional register with great alacrity lest enduring love translates into zombification. As Selina tells Jimmy in *28 Days Later* (2002): 'If someone gets

FIGURE 1.1 Zombie wedding, zombie parade, Adelaide, October 2012.

infected you've got between ten and twenty seconds to kill them. It might be your brother or your sister or your oldest friend. It makes no difference.'

When survivors in zombie fictions step back from their loved ones – with a cricket bat in hand – it's not just romantic love but the whole language and social organisation of love and family that is brought into question. This gesture – smashing in the head of the one you love – is repeated ad infinitum in zombie fictions as if its repetition could make habitable the intensity of the emotional violence that has become part of the everyday language of love. Sociologists argue the toss over whether the increased chaos of our emotional lives is creating new possibilities for 'pure relationships' (Giddens, 1992: 2), or new ways of making familial bonds, but zombie fictions deliver us into the raw violence of the divorce statistics. In a zombie fiction everyone is ultimately alone or at least bound for loneliness as one after another of the social bonds that bind them to others are lost to the zombie embrace. From my viewing point a decade ago, the 'zombie embrace' was an exercise in reality testing. Like all those survivors in a zombie fiction desperate to hold onto love or refind it in a new form, the cricket bat kept swinging. Love in the world of zombie is all about hungering for love but being hunted as meat: wanting love but ending up with blood on your hands.

German social theorist Ulrich Beck (Beck and Beck-Gernsheim, 2001: 203) calls the family 'a zombie category' arguing that it derives from nineteenth-century social institutions that have been superseded and yet still exert a powerful hold on our imaginary lives. In Beck and Beck-Gernsheim's (2001) thesis, we don't have a choice any longer to be 'for others' because our most intimate others are under an equal compulsion to be 'for themselves'. They posit an unerotic and asexual contradiction at work fuelling the battleground of sexual relations.

Individualisation is tearing intimate relations apart, forcing each of us to adopt individual solutions to life strategies; with the breakdown of traditional social identities the antagonism between men and women over gender roles emerges at the very heart of social relations:

> The ideal image conveyed by the labour market is that of the completely mobile individual regarding him/herself as a functioning flexible work unit, competitive and ambitious, prepared to disregard the social commitments linked to his/her existence and identity. This perfect employee fits in with the job requirements, prepared to move on whenever necessary.
> *(Beck and Beck-Gernsheim, 1995: 6)*

Survivors in zombie fictions are always moving on. They take the ideal of the unfettered mobile modern worker to new heights as they travel across the country stripped of their homes, families and communities. Families are the first to disintegrate in the zombie apocalypse. The film *28 Weeks Later* (2007) opens with a romantically engaged couple embracing as they prepare a communal meal in their boarded up farmhouse. Seconds later the zombies have battered down the doors and the man elects to save himself rather than defend his wife. The drama ensues from this first moment of betrayal when he chooses himself over the bonds of love and family. Reunited with his children they refuse to believe their mother is a zombie and return to their familial home to find her – in an ambivalent state. She is showing signs of zombification but is still human enough to entice the father to re-embrace her – giving her the opportunity for a revengeful bite. Zombified, the father becomes a rage-filled saturnine monster hunting down his children as if the only drive left in him is to destroy everything that grounds him to who he was and to who mattered to him in his earlier incarnation of a self bound to others. Sociologists of the family tend to quibble over just how faulty the modern family is contesting theoretic narratives such as Beck and

Beck-Gernsheim's (1995) as unduly pessimistic but zombie fictions are on the side of the pessimists.

Men in zombie films – even the human ones – tend to resume a primal state, a monstrous masculinity unbound by any collective or ethical imperative to serve social rather than singular needs. These monstrous men exercise a powerful dominion over women enforcing their return to domestic and sexual subservience, as if the apocalypse holds out the great promise that men will return to dominance and women to all fours. It's a bewildering and fearful scenario or an exciting promise – depending on which side of the sexual divide you fall on. But from my side the question is: Why does the past shadow the future in the form of a regression to this most primitive division of a patriarch in dominion over all other men and in possession of all women? Are dead social forms merely sleeping and waiting their moment to reawaken? What if women are once again sexual commodities to be traded by men, and men are once more a band of brothers cowering under the threat of a primal father? And what else might re-emerge from the past if all the dead social forms start walking again? In zombie fictions the aftermath of the zombie apocalypse is always anterior to the present and the future is already captured by the past.

Zombie combusts in a world of fragmented lives, failed intimacies, uncertain futures and phobic discourses. Unemployment, the collapse of the meanings and values in which one's identity is grounded, and the grief of a broken marriage – are the everyday crises of late modernity. In modernity, humans lose the consolation of religion and the shared identity of communal life, becoming 'individuated objects, isolated in space, and set in motion according to universal "laws of nature" devoid of intention or design, and blind to their consequences' (Ferguson, 1995: 10). In late modernity, even those forms of connectedness that modernity invented (nation, party, union, family), are shattering, leaving newly individuated subjects to quilt a meaningful life from a fragmenting yarn. Life in the late modern world holds few sureties. To be modern, as Zygmunt Bauman (2004) argues, is to be permanently at risk of falling prey to the unresolvable waste-disposal problem of modernity. It is to live in fear of being disembedded, atomised and at risk of being rendered waste: by redundancy; by the dissolution of bonds (families, communities, shared belief structures); or by the collapse that comes in the wake of radical, incessant change – of governments, states, borders, economies and environments.

As I write, another tsunami and another earthquake have hit Japan, a typhoon has killed over a thousand people in the Philippines, and a freak hurricane has devastated Auckland. Here in Adelaide the mercury mounts and, as we know from recent history, an incredibly dry country burns incredibly fast.[4] Few nations have been untouched by the global sweep of these environmental catastrophes – so portentous in their grim warning of future horror. To be alive today is to live permanently in what Ulrich Beck defines as a globalised risk society (Beck, 1992). The threatening forces of modernisation are no longer localised. Hazards which used to assault local environments now threaten the planet affecting all humanity and all human life – unforeseen, imperceptible and beyond rational control. Nuclear fission, radioactive waste, the destruction of environments, fires, floods and freak storms, the death of forests, the chemical hazards of mass commodity production create a *habitus* of risk in which even the world's most affluent are unable to protect themselves from the boomerang effect of unforeseen consequences and must dwell in a global state of doubt (Beck, 1992). Continuous war is the backdrop to this impending sense of doom. The twenty-first century has seen no end to the wars, death camps and gulags that killed 70 million in the horror-scapes of the twentieth century. The death toll continues to mount in a new century that opened with the longest war in US history (Bergen, 2011).

George Steiner (2001: 1–2) evokes this contemporary state as the end of the idea of beginning in a lost horizon of hope:

'We have no more beginnings ... inhumanity is, as far as we have historical evidence, perennial.' As in Benjamin's reading of Klee's Angelus Novus, Steiner (2001: 17) faces the past and sees only wreckage upon wreckage, but, unlike Benjamin, Steiner finds *futurity* itself – the if, shall and will of the future tense that the human species alone inhabits – in radical doubt:

> To repeat: violence, oppression, economic enslavement and social irrationality have been endemic in history, whether tribal or metropolitan. But the twentieth century has, owing to the magnitude of massacre, to the insane contrast between available wealth and actual *misère*, to the probability that thermonuclear and bacterial weapons could, in fact, terminate man or his environment, given to despair a new warrant. It has raised the distinct possibility or a reversal of evolution, of a systematic turnabout towards bestialisation. It is this which makes of Kafka's *Metamorphosis* the key fable of modernity or which, despite Anglo-Saxon pragmatism, renders plausible Camus' famous saying: 'the only serious philosophical question is that of suicide'.

For Steiner this crisis is grammatical. The future tense is indispensable to the 'language animal', it is what enables us to live in the face of the incomprehensibility of individual death; it is our 'passwords to hope', a semantic force which in every use negates the limits of mortality and inculcates the idea of hope through the idea of the future (Steiner, 2001: 5). But the vision is bleak.

Zombie fictional scenarios seem to concur. In lieu of the modernist maxim 'make it new' zombie fictional works drive the future into a cul-de-sac of no return. They hold out no promise, no hope, only the working through of what it is that makes the present an endless prolepsis of ruin. They seem to be inviting us into a pleasurable anticipation of the nothing that is coming as if reiterating the Lacanian quip, 'Why have something when you can have nothing?' And yet in this celebration of a future fall they turn on the present expostulating, critiquing, adumbrating with the energy of a utopic visionary as to why the present is failing the future.

Critics often find zombies' excursions into political critique burdensome as if zombie texts should stick to providing increasingly graphic and hyperreal scenes of exploding and disembowelling bodies. But political and social critique whether overt or covert, is as integral to the genre as is its splatterfest. Since its genesis in Romero's *Night of the Living Dead* (1968), the modern zombie genre has interspersed its prophetic vision of an apocalyptic future with a 'socio-political through-line' (cited in Yakir, 1977: 60). In its famous last scene viewers are thrown out of the absurd condition of being holed-up in an abandoned farmhouse surrounded by ravenous dead people to the horror-scape of 1960s American race relations. Ben, the film's black protagonist, survives a night of hell only to be shot and tossed on a bonfire by an all-white civil guard. In the Cuban film *Juan of the Dead* (2012), the government organises a manifestation against the 'dissidents' (i.e. the zombies) threatening to undermine the revolution but manifestation turns into a *monstration* as the red flags drown in blood. In *Zombie Strippers* (2008) the gyrations of rotten and decomposing women incite a sexual frenzy in their male onlookers and a desire on the part of the women onlookers to be the object of desire. Both men and women eagerly feed themselves to the zombies in a parody of today's pursuit of how to become the desirable thing. Even in its most excessive moments of violent dismemberment the zombie genre is puzzling through what it means to be human today.

This unfolding open-ended dialogue with catastrophe (past, present and future), gives zombies an almost imperial power *vis-à-vis* other genres. No less mobile in the fictional world than they are in modern discourse, the zombie genre has undergone a generic explosion cannibalising other genres and infiltrating fictional forms from literary classics to crime thrillers and historical romances. Generic zombie forms continue to proliferate, there are zombie westerns, zombie animé, zombie porn, zombie chic lit, zombie queer, to mention just a few. Few popular series on television today are without a zombie reference. In the medieval television fantasy *Game of Thrones* (2011) zombies, or 'white walkers', are the ghouls of a mythic past returning to threaten the present. In the fourth season of the drug thriller *Breaking Bad*, a series about a local chemistry teacher turned drug dealer, the protagonist Walter White finally blows up lethal drug baron Gus, but not without a horrifically mutilated Gus rising from the rubble in mimicry of the walking dead (in the episode 'Face Off', 2011). Even the acclaimed and multi-award-winning television drama *In Treatment* (2008) has its gesture to zombies, when the tension between troubled psychoanalyst Paul Western and his clinical supervisor and therapist Gina is diffused by Gina mimicking the psychoanalyst as a zombie mother.

Russian literary theorist Mikhail Bakhtin (1981) calls this kind of inter-generic chattering 'novelization', and argues that it occurs when a genre emerges that has an open-ended relation to the unfolding present. Bakhtin is writing specifically about the novel as a literary genre, but his theory of novelisation is particularly apt for conceptualising the kinds of infiltration and domination occurring within genres of both film and literature – when it comes to zombies. Indeed novelisation could be a synonym for zombification. According to Bakhtin (1981), a historically given drive exists within literature and is at work unpicking the artificial constraints of literature itself. Literary systems are comprised of canons that attempt to sustain rule-bound generic monologues but an opposing force – novelisation – defies monologic generic discourse (the formation of canons) and interrogates what any literary system will admit as literature (Bakhtin, 1981: xxx). What we think of as the novel, he argues, is simply the most condensed and distilled expression of this historical drive. Genre, in the narrow and historical sense of the term, is a single style involving a unified language system and conceived as a form acting like a container to hold and shape expression. In Antiquity, in the Classical Greek period and in the Golden Age of Roman literature, all the genres of 'high literature' were conceived as mutually reinforcing each other, and the whole of literature was understood as an organic unity formed from the totality of the genres. But the novel doesn't operate like this. According to Bakhtin (1981), the novel engulfs and ingests all other genres and non-literary forms of language; in this sense, it is not a genre in any traditional sense of the term. Whenever the novel arises, he argues, both in antiquity and the present, it is a completely new literary form that opens up new relations between literature, language and social reality. In response to the novel, other genres become more flexible and free, incorporate non-literary languages, become permeated with laughter, irony and self-parody, and enter into a semantic openness evolving a living relationship with reality and the open-ended present. It is this open-ended contact with the present that the novel appropriates and then spreads (Bakhtin, 1981). The novel then, in Bakhtin's (1981) understanding, is a self-critical, parodic and discursive genre that opens the hermetically sealed forms of the traditional genres into dialogue with unfolding modernity. This is where it derives its energy and vitality from, and why it so effectively devours older more stylised literary forms.

This description fits the kind of dialogic warfare occurring between the zombie genre and other generic forms. Think of Seth Graham-Smith's (2009: 7) *Pride and Prejudice and Zombies* with its devastating cannibalism of Austen's literary classic: 'It is a truth universally acknowledged that a zombie in possession of brains must be in want of more brains.' Even the most avid zombie fans would be hard pressed to defend this as a book worth reading – my interest barely survived the first page. But the book sold millions of copies and made its author a fortune because of its spectacular audacity – it ate one of the western world's most loved and respected classics. In doing so, it parodied Austen and the entire genre of romantic regency literature – and itself. Zombies devour things and here was a zombie novel devouring the classics. Max Brook's far more engaging novel, *World War Z* (2006) displays a similar novelising drive, directed in this instance to the genre of oral history. Inspired by Chicago journalist Stud Terkel's (1984) oral history of the Second World War, *The Good War*, the novel is a collection of oral interviews of veterans of the zombie war. Take away the zombie apocalyptic scenario and you could be reading a case study of Beck's theory of the globalisation of risk in late modernity. It is a thrilling book to read because it *actualises* risk theory, something that the fixed generic forms of the discourses of the social sciences just can't do.

If we follow Bakhtin's insight we can surmise that the zombie genre's success in infiltrating and dominating other genres has to do with its engagement with social reality. Like the left-wing movements of yesteryear, the zombie genre is *engagé*. *The Walking Dead* (2010), for example, unfolds like a question mark: what if the social contract collapses? What if men are no longer inhibited by the rule of law? What if the ties that bind us to our intimate others no longer hold? What if humans lose their humanity and become nothing more than their mute animal instincts? What if all the intimations of an uneasy future become Real? What if all boundaries and limits collapse? If the world is turned inside out and the dim past becomes our immediate future – what then? While exploring this game of hypotheticals *The Walking Dead* also plays a game with time. The 'what if' of a future time is shot through with fragments of a *now* and *then* no less horrific than the apocalyptic scenario playing out in fantasy. This is zombie time. In 'Secrets' (*The Walking Dead*, 2011b), episode six of the second season, survivors Shaun and Andrea drive out to a village in search of a missing child. They break into a house where the hallway has been walled in. Someone has made a stand here, hiding out in the secret part of the house. But no secret stands. These are zombies and they can smell life. The wall has a hole torn in it low to the floor as if a beast has broken through. Clambering on their knees through the hole, Andrea and Shaun are suddenly in a different kind of world. The bodies massed on the floor don't resemble the formulaic bodies of the devoured dead. These are bodies from a modern massacre: charred, rotting, flyblown. We are suddenly catapulted from the unfolding story of the missing girl into the killing fields of Rwanda, Bosnia, Cambodia. We know these dead bodies; they are familiar to us. We have seen them on our television screens as they are disinterred from the mass graves of modernity. But interrupting the pleasurable weekly instalment of a zombie TV series makes them momentarily new, REAL, unassimilated. And then attention shifts. The zombies have wind of Andrea and Shaun and a horde is massing at an open roller door. We are back in an imagined apocalyptic future freed from the present and its cast out and cast off time zones.

The Walking Dead is the most popular television programme in the history of cable TV (screening its third season at the time of writing) bringing a definitive end to the idea that zombies belong in the fringe. In a brilliant coup, it combines the strong narrative lure of serialised TV with the normally restricted horizon of a zombie film, the bleak end-time of the zombie apocalypse. Zombie films usually leave their protagonists in a bleak unreconciled landscape of unfolding horror; the viewer never knows what ultimately happens and the narrative scenario remains unresolved. But, apart from this one generic departure, *The Walking Dead* is generically quite tame. Rather than attempting to twist an already bent genre, a number of generic variations play out across the episodes while never straying too far from iconic zombie themes. Zombies in *The Walking Dead* have few surprises. They shuffle, walk *and run*; sometimes they reanimate in seconds, sometimes over hours. They are unanimously hungry, unremittingly violent and, thus far, show little sign of adaptation, intelligence or rehabilitative potential. It is as if the directors want to keep afloat a mainstream zombie that integrates some of its generic variations while not deflecting from the main focus of the series, which is an interrogation of morality *face à face* the collapse of sociality.

But what is a zombie?

Contemporary philosophical and cultural discourse abounds with explanations of what the zombie is and what it means. In *Looking Awry* Slavoj Žižek (1992: 22–3) equates the zombies of Romero's *Night of the Living Dead* with Antigone and the ghost of Hamlet's father, seeing them as 'sufferers, pursuing their victims with an awkward persistence, coloured by a kind of infinite sadness'. The key to understanding zombies in this reading is the Lacanian idea of a form of pure drive that is caught up in an incessant demand that persists even beyond the grave. Caught 'between two deaths' (Žižek, 1992: 22) such figures signify a symbolic disturbance: 'The return of the dead is a sign of disturbance in the symbolic rite, in the process of symbolisation; the dead return as collectors of some symbolic debt' (Žižek, 1992: 23). But in another context Žižek argues that

> at the most elementary level of our human identity we are all zombies and our "higher" and "free" human activities can only take place insofar as they are founded on the reliable functioning of our zombie habits; being a zombie is a zero level of humanity, the inhuman/mechanical core of humanity.
>
> *(Gabriel and Žižek, 2009: 100)*

Marina Warner (2006: 367) understands zombies as 'figures of the world's unspeakableness. They embody that nullity and disaffection that makes the untellable story of the world possible to bear.' But Warner (2006: 368) also recognises the plasticity of the figure:

> The term's meanings keep twisting and turning in the utterance of different parties, now a weapon to put distance between us and them, an insult, an estranging label, a joke, a bond to draw us closer together and finally a mirror of a certain common fear of numbness and loss.

Warner is right. Explaining zombies through the lens of a particular cultural theory can help us understand aspects of the figurative, generic and socio-political resonance of zombies, but zombies are plastic, amorphous and contradictory.

Lately I'm more bewildered by zombies than comforted by them. When I say bewildered, I'm not suggesting that there aren't highly plausible ways of understanding why zombies have become so central to the contemporary imaginary, but, rather, that there are genuinely bewildering questions provoked by the emergence of zombies. Zombies are demonstrating an extraordinary capacity to transport fluidly from genre to genre, from the apocalyptic future to the already survived past, and in and out of fictional form. Zombies are ubiquitous. They can be found in just about any genre or discourse and as they move sinuously across the cultural landscape they keep morphing, taking on ever new and ever more bizarre associations. I'm intrigued by what is it about these shambolic metaphors of death that makes them so compelling for people today. Zombies would appear to be unthinkable, the ultimate nightmare of a world devoured by the dead, and yet more and more often this horror-scape provides a form of figurative capture for the way things are. But it's 'complicated' to borrow Avery Gordon's (1997: 3) term. This is why I want to leave the question of what a zombie is – open. Zombies don't belong in a neat theoretical box; they're famously gate-crashing creatures. Embedding in the contemporary imagination as the new face of contemporary horror they also keep alive buried histories. A vision of an apocalyptic future they evoke the repressed memory of what was and what is unfolding – *now*, on the dark side of the mirror. There is nothing simple about the mobile and plastic phantasm, metaphor, ritual, text, genre, identification and discourse – that is zombie. As much an event in language and ritual as they are in fantasy, zombies defy systematising. Understanding the way they speak to us, the way we speak through them requires asking questions and seeing where they lead you.

Zombie semantics: 'She was given a zombie'

Only a few years ago zombie was a word referring to a finite number of traits and characteristics. According to the *New Oxford Dictionary of English* (1998) a zombie, 'is a corpse said to be revived by witchcraft, esp. in certain African and Caribbean religions'. It had the further informal meaning of 'a person who is or appears lifeless, apathetic, or completely unresponsive to their surroundings'. It had only one adjectival form, 'zombie-like', and one verbal form, 'to zombify', meaning to deprive of energy or vitality. The 1998 online *Oxford English Dictionary* included a further meaning: a term of Canadian military slang in the war of 1939–45, used as a derogatory nickname for men conscripted for home defence. It added the further adjectival forms of zomboid and zomboiesque. Later additions of the OED online included zombie as a term in computing for 'a computer of which another person has gained control without the knowledge of the user, usually as one of many used concertedly to send spam email or to bombard a targeted web site with data so as to make the site inaccessible to other users'. By 2001, the *American Oxford Dictionary* had expanded its meanings to include, 'a tall mixed drink consisting of several kinds of rum, liquor and fruit juice'. But zombie gathered meanings as the first decade of the twenty-first century unfolded. In *Urban Dictionary* (2013) a zombie is: a slow girl who likes smart guys and makes them dumb by sucking out their brains; someone who is so dishevelled and unkempt that they look like they have arisen from the grave; crack or someone who is addicted to crack; a type of computer virus that sends numerous amounts of useless packets to a computer or a server and floods it to crash its connection; an internet thread that has become reanimated after being dormant for some time; a previously banned forum user who creates a new account for the sole purposes of causing trouble or being a troll; a model of conformist citizen; a slang term for potent marijuana; a person who lacks originality and just goes with the flow of society; a person inebriated to the point of only being able to engage in basic human functions; an electronic device that has suddenly started working again; democrats; someone who does absolutely nothing during sexual intercourse; a non-vegetarian; someone who eats flesh; a stupid person; a lazy worker; a drone; someone infected with STDs; a sexual act 'where a man ejaculates onto a female's eyes so that they put their hands out looking for a towel like a zombie, i.e. she was given a "zombie"'. Zombie's many meanings include an underbelly of dark and dirty sexuality, this being just one of the many forms of sexual acts and sexual classifications that are defined as 'zombie': 'Adam gave Adriana the zombie this morning she fell down ... full thriller style' (*Urban Dictionary*, 2013). Meanings cluster along such pathways but meaning itself remains anomalous. Zombie is no longer just a fictional form, a sub-genre or fantasy-scape, nor is it restricted to video games, comic strips and horror films. Within the space of just a decade, zombie has morphed from a word of finite meanings into a mass metaphor. Zombie is much more than a word defining a thing; it is a way of making meaning; an endlessly digressing metaphor gathering associations as it slips from objects to discourses to things – at a far remove from Haiti or Hollywood.

Zombie as metaphor

There is a long tradition in western thinking of regarding figurative language as antithetical to knowledge. New theoretical paradigms emerging in the later decades of the twentieth century went some way to redressing this, but the methodological barbed wire of the social sciences still gets in the way of understanding the centrality of metaphors to social life, despite a large body of anthropological writing on the way lived experience is mediated by metaphor. An antiquated view of metaphor persists often taking the form of criticising arguments that deploy metaphors as resting on 'mere allegory'. But the 'mere allegory' of zombie is hard at work in the social world.

The idea of figurative language as a deviant use of language without cognitive value has its origins in Aristotle's (1996: 34) *Poetics*, where metaphor is defined as 'the application of a noun which properly belongs to something else. The transference being either from genus to species, from species to genus, or from species to species or by analogy.' Conceived as mere literary devices and creative embellishments, the slipperiness of metaphors was seen to get in the way of knowledge. The idea of metaphor as an obfuscating use of language reached a high point with the empiricist philosophers of the sixteenth and seventeenth centuries and their attempts to create an objective language of knowledge unmediated by subjective interference. Locke, as de Man argues, conceived of figurative language as a disruptive power with the potential to subvert the congruency between words and things. Locke attempted to relegate the figure to 'a disruptive scandal, like the appearance of a real woman in a gentleman's club where it would only be tolerated as a picture, preferably naked (like the image of Truth) framed and hung on the wall' (de Man, 1984: 197). He tried to develop a theory of language in which simple ideas and ideas of substance represented real entities in the world but, as de Man argues, rather than mapping the entities of the world in an identical relationship, Locke's 'simple ideas' are in fact figures, slipping in an endless series of translations.

Since the publication of I.A. Richards's (1936) and Max Black's (1954) seminal works on metaphor many scholars have argued that scientific language, presumed to be language at a literal zenith, is in fact both figurative at the level of the sentence and at the level of narrative emplotment. Johnson (1981), Blinkley (1974), Cohen, (1976) and Lakoff and Johnson (1980) argued that the human conceptual system is metaphorically structured and that even the most literal expressions rely on conventional metaphors, such as the use of spatial metaphors in everyday language. Perhaps most importantly, Ricoeur (1978) argued that metaphor not only conveys meaning but is also possibly the principle behind meaning. In other words, metaphors, as Lakoff and Johnson (1980) have pointed out, are what we live by.

Scholars are not exempt from this. As metaphor, zombie has colonised the natural, social and human sciences. In entomology, zombies are viruses that invade insects and compel them to act in suicidal ways (Kuchment, 2011). In biology, they are parasites that compel their hosts to behave in ways adventitious to their resident zombies (Rozen, 2011). In astronomy, a star becomes a zombie by appearing to die in a supernova while continuing to live on (Nature, 2012). In neurology, neural networks and pathways cause unconscious and automatic forms of zombie behaviour (Crick and Koch, 2001; Ratliff, 2005). In IT, computers are zombies hijacked by hackers and set loose in the corporate world (Spring, 2005). In economics, zombies proliferate faster than marks in the Weimar Republic (Domm, 2012). There are zombie banks, zombie economic theories and zombie policies (Quiggin, 2011). (Obama's health care reform is 'like a zombie out of *Night of the Living Dead*' (Miller cited in *The Economist*, 2010: para. 7)). In fact, the entire US economy has become a zombie. According to some economists, the US government's economic bailout of private businesses in the aftermath of the world financial crisis reanimated businesses that should have been allowed to die, creating a zombie economy falsely animated by government largesse and causing havoc in society as real businesses do battle with their zombie competitors.[5] In this context, zombie carries the association of an unnatural intervention in a natural death. Death has been thwarted leading to a threatening state of disequilibrium as the living battle for survival with the undead. But the US economy is also 'zombie-like' because of its stalled recovery (Censky, 2012). It won't get up and walk – though this is exactly what zombies do. In Japan, however, zombie firms stagger back to life (Fukada and Nakamura, 2011). Democrats are zombies but so too are Republicans (Nature, 2012). In the social sciences, the zombie metaphor catapulted into fame when Ulrich Beck (Beck and Beck-Gernsheim, 2001) argued that the sociological imagination was haunted by zombie categories, concepts derived from experiences of nineteenth-century modernity that refused to die. But Beck's concept of zombie categories failed to control the metaphor's spread – even amongst social scientists. Daniel Drezner (2011) recast contemporary international relations theory through the lens of the zombie threat. As he explains, zombie apocalyptic scenarios have more in common with threats posed by terrorists, hackers and tsunamis than the state-centric theories of standard international relations. In the health sciences, the construction of people with Alzheimer's disease as zombies has become a serious matter for health workers (Behuniak, 2011), which the *Journal of Clinical Nursing* complicates by publishing a clinical article on how to best provide nursing care in a zombie apocalypse (Stanley, 2012).

To ask what a zombie is, then, is to ask what do zombies mean and how do they mean? One answer to this question is that zombie is the word on everybody's lips to express all forms of being, behaving and operating that lack a little *je ne sais quoi*. You no longer need to know anything about zombie films or computer games to use zombie as a generalised metaphor for everything that is wrong with contemporary life. It is not just humans (singular and en masse) that lack this *je ne sais quoi*, but environments, political structures, social institutions, behaviours and systems. Cropping up everywhere as a noun used to modify other nouns, zombie connotes lack, but the meanings given to this lack are without consistency. As we have seen, even within the one discursive sphere zombie means different things. In architecture, for example, zombie buildings are untenanted office blocks, condominiums and shopping centres that were built before the world financial crisis and are now set to plunge the US financial system into financial chaos (Spolar and Sebert, 2012). Here, zombie implies a potent absence. But zombie buildings are also the products of show-off architects who design glass boxes that do not speak to their environments. Mute and soulless these zombies are not potent but threateningly impotent (D'Alterio, 2012). In both cases, the adjectival noun implies an inner absence with the power to act upon us in negative ways, but the form this action takes is open ended. Zombie is a word with amorphous properties. As an adjectival noun zombie retains the agency of a verb; it both describes and acts. But zombie is also a state of being. Both things and people can look, act, appear, seem, feel or be zombified. In this sense, zombie is both a property that can be possessed and a lack that is at the same time a mode of action. And zombies can be anything! Zombies are voters that lack acuity, institutions that refuse to dissolve and litigants that lack volition. But, to pose another contradiction, these agents of lack also have use-value. Zombie sells. Toyota cashed in on the zombie apocalypse by advertising their Toyota Corolla as an effective shield against zombies (Stanley, 2010). You can play zombie soccer, zombie Lego and farm zombies, or buy everyday objects distorted to meet the zombie menace – from zombie repellent umbrellas to zombie toothpicks. You name it and you'll find its commoditised zombie form on the web. I scored three out of three with zombie elephants, zombie skydivers and zombie mushrooms.

Zombie is the word on everyone's lips because zombie *as metaphor* condenses elements of the present that we most need, and are least able, to think about. If we approach zombies as mere fictional constructs or understand the zombie metaphor – as mere allegory – then we entirely miss what is going on with zombies today. Metaphors are ways of making meaning and as such they are vehicles for thought. Metaphors travel, carrying meanings from one semantic place to another – boundary riding can't stop the over-leaping logic of a good metaphor. Zombie is a metaphor that enables 'us' – a mass us; an undifferentiated, transcultural, global us – to think the impossibility of now. Zombie is not a metaphor contrived for scholars (although clearly scholars are interpellated by it). It is a mass metaphor detonating in the world of popular culture and it is from this vantage point that it travels. Fluid in its capacity to move from realm to realm, at the same time it fixes diverse experiences within its semantic constellation. The hybrids of the semantic world, metaphors loves *mesalliance* – and zombie as metaphor links opposites: death and life; passivity and aggressivity; drive and enslavement; discontinuity and continuity; love and hate; consumption and revulsion; the individual and the mass; self and other; an apocalyptic future and a repressed past. It condenses time making the future now and the past return. Through the figure of zombie all that is past, dead and buried looms up in a future time that is upon us. Zombie is a figure that empties meaning while proliferating it. It critiques, questions, interrogates the way things are while bleakly laying out the impossibility of them being otherwise.

There is no easy answer to the question, what is a zombie. But one way we can understand the mobility of zombies today is as a particular kind of metaphor: a *metatrope* – a figure that binds together other figures in a dense network of meanings. Zombie is a metatrope that has metastasised, invading other metaphors and tropes and binding them together in permeating networks of figures in an ever-expanding semantic take-over. And zombie – as metaphor – is not something you want to be, which brings into question what all those 'wannabe' zombies are doing at zombie parades going on all around the world.

2
THE COLLECTIVE ZOMBIE

This brings me back to the parade and to the even more curious question of what happens to 'zombie as metaphor' when it takes to the street as a public spectacle. In zombie parades, groups of people who have entered imaginatively into a fictional form, collectively create a social ritual out of its imaginary constituents. This movement from narrative to social enactment, from the imaginary and symbolic world of fiction to the corporeal world of bodies, acts, rituals and performances creates a new kind of collective manifestation. Consecrated by rituals of performance and pantomime the zombie parade is a collective event that transforms a private act of viewing zombie films or playing zombie games into a visible, public and global manifestation of a collective identification.

From humble beginnings as an event to promote a horror film festival in Sacramento, California, in 2001, zombie parades and festivals are becoming mainstream events attracting thousands of participants in cities across the world. Zombie websites record this escalating tally as if the rise in active zombiism underwrites the veracity of the zombie vision – 9,800 in Mexico in 2011 (*ABC News*, 2011); an estimated 15,000 in Brisbane, Australia, in October 2011 (Zombie, 2011); 12,000 in Santiago, Chile, in October 2012 (Arsova, 2012); 15,000 in October 2012 in Asbury Park, New Jersey (Columbus, 2012); 25,000 in Buenos Aires, Argentina, in October 2012 (Murch *et al.*, 2012) and so on.

In comparison to the world's big religious festivals and parades, with participation by hundreds of thousands of people, the zombie parades are small affairs, but they mark the transformation of zombie from a fictional genre into zombie as a social form. Zombies incite forms of identification and pleasures that are moving off the screen and into the street, and these street events are fanned by the rise and rise of the zombie genre. Google trends reveal that web search interest in zombie headlines has risen steeply from a search index of 11 in 2004 (out of a maximum of 100) to 88 in October 2012 (Google, 2012). The cultural spread of these fans is another zombie surprise. Zombie fans cross languages, cultures and nations. In the period 2004–12 Indonesia scored 100, Mongolia 64, the United States 74 and Australia 56. Phillipinos (94) are more interested in zombies than the French (35), but in the UK (53) there is far less interest than in Canada (61) (Google, 2012).

We, the zombie

Marxist philosopher Alain Badiou argues that the political demonstrations of the twentieth century had the function of creating a collective subject by endowing a 'we' with a body:

> The gathering of bodies into a single moving material form is intended to say: 'we' are here, and 'they' (the powerful, the others, those who do not enter into the composition of the 'we') should be afraid and take our existence into consideration.
>
> *(Badiou, 2005: 106–7)*

For Badiou, the demonstrations made visible the belief in a 'we' able to transform everything, a collective determination to transform a collection 'of noughts' of isolated individuals into a body that endows itself with the power of insurrection. He contrasts this with the celebrations of the first decade of the twenty-first century, which he characterises as harmless and consensual (Badiou, 2005: 107). But aren't zombie marches and parades also an overt manifestation of a collective power that *theatricalises* the power of insurrection – albeit in forms radically unlike the insurrections of the twentieth century? Zombie marches don't have an evident political strategy but they have a collective intention and one that we need to understand outside the rhetoric of the old Left.

The old Left promised its adherents a collective identity under the umbrella of the fundamental fantasy that humans, in particular and en masse, could be created anew by transforming the structural contradictions inherent in the social relations governing the division of labour. But participating in this fantasy delivered its adherents into socio-political structures that involved an endemic hunting out and persecution of difference. Milan Kundera (1978) captures this with the image of socialism as a circle dance of seemingly simple steps but with one tricky move: a high flung back kick that knocks out the dancers so that the circle keeps getting smaller and smaller. In all those moments when the circle dance closed – in the gulags, camps and killing fields – this dance translated fantasy into slag heaps of human waste. In effect, this is what Badiou's rhetoric is doing when he *idealises* the experience of dwelling inside the fantasmatic causes of the twentieth century: 'From the inside, the century was lived as epic and heroic' (Badiou, 2005: 33). We can only belong to this 'inside' if we read this sentence like an end-stopped line, its meaning complete in itself. In doing so, we forget the way the 'century', to borrow Badiou's term, *worked through* its fundamental fantasy viscerally and affectively: in trade route and garbage piles, in toxic events and digital revolutions, in the freedom struggles of the colonised, in traumatic repetitions visited on couch after couch, in the tracked veins of the counter-culture, in the fragmenting worlds of refugees and of bourgeois nuclear families ... individuals en masse 'worked though' the fantasies underpinning the ideologies and causes of the century – as they floundered in the detritus left in the wake of fantasy.

Unsurprisingly, zombie marchers would seem to belong to a different public altogether, one manifesting the end point of the utopic fantasies that caused such mayhem and destruction in the twentieth century. Taking to the street, zombie publics manifest a discordant history that is the very antithesis of the idealising logics of twentieth-century political movements. Zombie publics are not a collective 'we' manifesting the capacity to reverse the order of history, but a 'we' identifying with fictional works that assume a future end-point to the present and mobilise visions of the present as irretrievably doomed. The zombie vision is unrelievedly pessimistic; even when hilarious there's no escape from the melancholia of a zombie landscape. Thousands of people lurching down the street dripping with gore and calling for brains are signifying negativity. It might not be the idea of a revolutionary fraternity that draws them together, but somewhere in the mix of this festive blood-scape is the idea of an all-encompassing social rottenness. Chaotically nihilistic, lacking any political credo zombie demonstrators nevertheless gesture towards a world awry. Pessimistically *playful* and critically celebratory, they defy judgment in terms of the old polarities of revolution and reaction.

To begin with, zombie street festivals seem first and foremost to be about play. They transform the street into an arena of creative exuberance and pageantry warping and twisting the fantasy figures of generations past into new avatars of horror. As a form of street theatre, zombie festivals forge a community around play reclaiming make-believe as the property of ordinary people. The mediatised spectacles of the zombie genre might provide a guiding star to their pageantry, but the costumes, face painting, masks and masquerade are home-grown. In Adelaide, the zombie festival resonated with the emancipatory joyfulness of *Mardi Gras* and seemed to be aspiring to the transgressive spirit of the world's great carnivals in its tumultuous display of grotesquery. But it had none of the shared cosmology of carnival, or *Kanaval*, nor did it fit with the way 'festival' or 'carnival' is often understood by sociologists as a form of transient social solidarity providing a euphoric moment of voice and community to marginalised and disenfranchised peoples. The only unifying thread in this chaotic assemblage of characters was the inherently violent and destabilising figure of zombie. The figure itself – the collective body taking form on the street – was a deliriously euphoric pageantry of violence, an apocalyptic vision of death stalking the present as it refigured the past through its own macabre lens. Whatever desire, inner necessity, affect, creative intent or identification had motivated this group of strangers into playing the game of zombie en masse, on the street they performed a hellish vision. Yet all the paraphernalia of the old Left formed part of its pageantry. The chants, 'What do we want? Brains; When do we want them? Now', the slogans 'eat the rich' and the blood-soaked red flags were part of the visual montage of this new collective face of insurrection.

Provenance

Zombies have their own embedded revolutionary semantics but it's one that falls outside of revolutionary heroics. Deriving from the revolutionary history of Haiti zombies are not the heroes of the revolution but its failures. In Haiti, there's nothing funny, fantastic or entertaining about zombies, as ethnographer Wade Davis writes: 'In Haiti the fear is not of being harmed by zombies as much as becoming one' (Davis, 1988: 191). In their original embedded form they function as allegories of a violent and *de-individuated* past, reminding the living that there is no greater horror than being stripped of the two indivisible traits of the human – sociality and individuality.

All former colonies have their own (usually elided) histories of anguish and shame, but the French made brutality an art form in Saint-Domingue, one of the richest and most profitable of plantation colonies. Before the astonishing event of the slave revolution, in which armies of rebel slaves led by Toussaint L'Ouverture defeated Napoleon's troops and formed the independent black Republic of Haiti in 1804, indigenous Indians, convicts, indentured servants and poor whites kidnapped from Europe, and hundreds of thousands of West Africans – were treated with utter brutality:

> The documented excesses of certain owners almost defy belief. One slave was kept in chains for 25 years. A notorious planter always carried a hammer and nails with him just so as to be prepared to hang from the trees the severed ears of those he punished. Other common tortures included spraying the flesh with boiling cane syrup, sewing the lips together with brass wire, castration and sexual mutilation of both men and women, live burial, binding men – their skin glazed with molasses – across the paths of ants, enclosing people in barrels studded with inward-protruding nails, and stuffing the anus with gunpowder which was then ignited; the latter practice was common enough to give rise to the expression, 'blasting a black's ass'.
> *(Fouchard cited in Davis, 1988: 215)*

Haitian zombies are depositaries of the traumatic memory of this past kept alive through a generalised social fear of being made zombie, and more recently through the pageantry of Haitian Kanaval:

> The *zonbi* is an object of fear used by secret societies who are believed to have the power to raise the dead. The *zonbi*

is a mnemonic menace, a reminder of a time when slavery attempted to remake humans as lifeless labourers.

(Smith, 2010: 80)

The etymological origins of the word zombie's various attributions include the indigenous Arawak culture of Haiti (jumbies or juppy/duppy), the African Bonda language (zumbi), the Mitsogho of Gabon (ndzumbi) and the Kongo word (nzambi) (Davis, 1988). Hans W. Ackerman and Jeanine Gauthier (1991) provide detailed etymological and folkloric evidence that zombies travelled to Haiti via the slave route and detail a long history of similar beliefs in the reanimation of the dead and theft of the soul across both the Caribbean and Africa. They're less convinced, however, by the large body of writing documenting how zombies became integrated into Haitian culture in the aftermath of the slave revolution. But as Kyle William Bishop (2010: 42) argues, their establishment of the zombie as 'an immigrant to the West Indies' is 'an observation that underscores the essential role played by imperial colonisation and slavery in the creation of the modern-day zombie'.

Most scholars agree that Haitian zombies have their specific genesis in slavery but there is little agreement about whether zombies are mythical or real, how they are created, or what their relationship is to the Voodou religion. Unsurprisingly, given the political, racial, and epistemological stakes in play, when it comes to Haitian zombies scholarship is combative and highly contentious:

> Do zombies actually exist? On one side have been ranked the intellectuals, scholars, and government officials who have dogmatically – and perhaps understandably – consigned the phenomenon to fable (Bourguignon 1959; Laroche 1976; Mars 1945, 1947; Métraux 1972; Herskovits 1975; Leyburn 1941; Courlander 1960), and on the other educated individuals – foreign and Haitian physicians and

> psychiatrists, missionaries, writers, and reporters – who claim that at least some of the accounts are legitimate (Hurston 1981; Dewisme 1957; Douyon 1980; Diederich 1983; Kline pers.com.; Lehman pers.com.).
>
> *Davis (1988: 61–2)*

Scholarly accounts of Haitian zombification practices differ widely, but most scholars accept zombification (at least figuratively) as carrying the threat of a return to enslavement.[1] In Haiti in the 1930s, writer and ethnographer Zora Neale Hurston (2009) pieced together elements of the practice of zombification leading her to separate it from the religion of Voodou. To her informants, the secret cults that practised zombification were more like the mafia than the Houngans, the priests of Voodou. Upper-class Haitians attempted to dissuade her from listening to peasants' stories of zombies, arguing that such talk was 'mere allegory' derived from the poetic and figurative propensities of Haitian peasants and their mythical traditions. But Hurston found that the upper class no less than the peasantry feared becoming zombie:

> The upper class Haitians fear too, but they do not talk about it so openly as do the poor. But to them also it is a horrible possibility. Think of the fiendishness of the thing. It is not good for a person who has lived all his life surrounded by a degree of fastidious culture, loved to his last breath by family and friends, to contemplate the probability of his resurrected body being dragged from the vault – the best that love and means could provide, and set to toiling ceaselessly in the banana fields, working like a beast, unclothed like a beast, and like a brute crouching in some foul den, in the few hours allowed for rest and food. From an educated, intelligent being to an unthinking, unknowing beast. Then there is the helplessness of the situation. Family and friends cannot rescue the victim

because they do not know. They think the loved is sleeping peacefully in his grave. They may motor past the plantation where the zombie who was once dear to them is held captive often and again its soulless eyes may have fallen upon them without thought or recognition.
(Hurston, 2009: 180)

Hurston's accounts of secret mafia-type societies exercising a fearful dominion over Haitians were highly controversial, but later ethnographic research by Wade Davis supported many of her claims. Davis's (1988) research into zombification, albeit also highly controversial, provides some of the most convincing elucidation of how Haitian zombification occurs pharmaceutically (etically), and what it means (emically) within the belief systems of Haitian religious, social and political practices. He identifies both spiritual and material zombies but his research focuses primarily on the latter, the *corps cadaver*. Davis (1988), like Hurston, argues that zombies are pitiful miscreants who have been buried in a trance induced by a poison that gives the appearance of death, and are then raised from the grave, displaced far from their homes, and set to work in perpetuity as mindless semi-comatose slaves. To create a zombie, he writes, the *ti bon ange,* the part of the human soul responsible for individuality is taken by a powerful Bokor: 'it is the *ti bon ange* that moulds the individual sentiments within each act. It is one's aura, and the source of all personality, character and will power' (Davis, 1988: 186–7). Taking the *ti bon ange* from the victim makes them mere flesh, a body stripped of its morality, its will, its selfhood.

In *Passage of Darkness* Davis (1988) retraces the ground of his earlier famous ethnography *The Serpent and the Rainbow* (Davis, 1985) to provide a more sustained ethnographic, sociological, psychological and pharmacological analysis of zombification. In this second study he contextualises etic causes (poisoning by substances including tetrodotoxins) within the emic belief systems of Voodou that encode the experiences of poisoning with the signification of becoming zombie. His research into the Bizango sect leads to the hypothesis that secret societies that formed the basis of the revolutionary slave movement continued as an underground social system of governance in Haiti. These groups defend the space of the revolution and its communities from social disorder. Zombification, he argues, is a form of supreme sanction issued by the tribunals of the secret societies against those who have profoundly offended social law. Katherine Smith makes a similar contention:

> Bizango has functioned as an institution of policing and justice, a role it has filled in the void of a stable and competent state. Part of the threat posed by the society is the ability to appropriate and manipulate the power of the coloniser. Bizango has the capability not only to inflict mystical death, but also to implement fates even worse, like transforming humans into mindless chattel.
> *(Smith, 2010: 80)*

Zombification entails living death. Once zombified, the victim is permanently exiled from society, dead to all prior relations, and bound over to toil endlessly, casting them back into the abjection of the slave condition. Thus the zombie is a figure that doubles the trauma of the past. It signifies a past that awaits; a past to which one can always be returned if, through transgression, one loses the right to being an individuated subject in a free society.

Mobile metaphors

Zombies walked out of Haiti in texts such as William Seabrook's (1989 [1929]) *The Magic Island,* in plays such as Kenneth Webb's *Zombie* (1932), and films such as *White Zombie* (1932) and *I Walked with a Zombie* (1943). Mutating as they came, these soul-starved beings carried the fused signs of enslavement, cultural desecration and revolutionary emancipation, mixed up with the fulminating fantasies of their western progenitors.

Accounts of the migration of zombies into the west tend to focus on how Hollywood zombies mire an African–Caribbean religious tradition in colonial fantasies of a primitive and cannibalistic black magic. The colonial fear that the abusive treatment of slaves would rebound produced fantastic images of Voodou rituals and zombie practices. Alfred Métraux (1959: 15) describes Seabrook's fanciful constructions of Voodou as a blood-maddened, sex-maddened, God-maddened saturnalia and suggests the source of these fantasies is the violent madness of slavery itself: 'Man is never cruel and unjust with impunity: the anxiety which grows in the minds of those who abuse power often takes the form of imaginary terrors and demented obsessions.'

As significant as these fears and projections are, they're not the only input feeding into the zombie matrix as it takes generic form in the west. Even in the most exotic, racialised and sexualised constructions of Voodou sorcerers and bloody rituals (see Kee, 2011) memory *insists*. In colonial texts there is always a residue, a stain, an affective discordance that troubles and buckles myth making. Zombie texts are no different.

Born out of the wasted landscapes of colonial Saint-Domingue, the western filmic zombie carries the symbolic traces of the abjection of slavery, its overthrow *and* its return, and projects this back into the western world dramatised in the form of the zombie chewing its way through cultures and peoples – rendering everything in its path mere animal matter. Romero didn't create the modern zombie; he *resurrected* it under the sign of a new avatar. The flesh consuming violence of the modern zombie evokes the real *gluttony* of French colonials feeding off slave labour just as contemporary zombie scenarios of modern cities laid waste evoke modernity's repressed history as waste-makers of the cultures and peoples of the colonised world. As Zygmunt Bauman argues in *Wasted Lives,* waste making is an inseparable component of modernity and its project of *order building*. Modernisation made over the world, categorising earlier modes of social and economic organisation and their subjects as out of place, unfit, undeveloped and undesirable (Bauman, 2004). This excremental logic played itself out globally in the production of sites of order (the metropolitan centres of the modern world) and sites of chaos (the dumping grounds of modernity's waste products). In the European modern imagination, colonial spaces existed only for what they might deliver (raw materials) and what they might receive (excess humans). The structural inequality between the modern metropolises and their colonial outposts allowed the inherent disorder of modernity's ordering drives to be externalised, as humans surplus to the requirements of the new industrial modes of production were shipped out of site (Bauman, 2004). But modernity bites back; refuse returns in human and inhuman forms.

Migrating from Haiti zombies might have hitched a ride on some western orientalising exotica but they brought with them – under the cover of the text – all the refuse of colonialism. Zombies carry the traces of their horrific masters; they are ransackers, ravaging societies, devouring custom and tradition with blind indifference to all they destroy. In the zombie vision of an apocalyptic future the past returns in a new mutation, which gathers up the horror and the anguish of the past, its victims and its most vile antagonists, into a new figure that casts all before it into a state of de-individuated waste. Speaking about *Night of the Living Dead* (1968), Romero suggests that he conceived of this first modern zombie film as a return to the original zombies of Haiti. In his words, 'It's a return to what the zom-bie was in the beginning: Lugosi always lived in a castle while the zombies went out to pick sugar-cane' (cited in Yakir, 1977: 60). It's a somewhat confused statement suggesting that Romero blurs filmic and Haitian history, but what is clear is that Romero has in mind the legacy of slavery incumbent in the figure of the zombie. *Night of the Living Dead* is often conceived as the moment when Haitian zombies are superseded by the modern Hollywood zombie, but this critical moment of generic creation marks a return to an embedded history. Present if not uttered, these suspended contexts of meaning *sound*, to borrow Jacques Lacan's (1966: 154) analogy, 'along the several staves of a score'.

Contemporary Zombie fictional works often bring these suspended contexts of meaning into the light and make the link between zombies and slavery explicit. *Zombie Wars* (2008) begins with a line of shackled women being driven along by their zombie masters. Raised from birth as farmed meat and as slaves for the zombie plantation, the women are as mute and asocialised as the zombies. Dressed in rags of erstwhile designer clothes, and still sporting shaved legs, plucked eyebrows and the orthodontically adjusted teeth of middle America, these all-white slaves are rescued by a band of rebel humans hiding out in the jungle. The whites righteously throw off their slave masters in a massacre that leaves the plantation strewn with the corpses of slaughtered zombies. It's a classic inversion. The lived experience of a colonised group is assumed by the colonisers and restaged in a scenario in which they become the new victims of oppression. But somehow it lacks the theatrical punch of the Haitian *lansetkòd* who, in Kanaval, perform the actual revolutionary inversion of colonial history in the slave revolution. These terrifying figures, their skin shimmering with cane-syrup and molasses and sporting phallic bulls' horns charge the crowd with their whips cracking. Smith (2010: 80) cites Nabot Power, head of the largest group of performing *lansetkòd*:

> The ropes were used in the revolution. They tied up people who mistreated people. They mistreated us – they beat us, they hit us, they made us miserable – the colonisers did. Now the rope, we used it like in Mardi Gras to sneak up behind someone and *blap!*, tie them down, and beat them, What they did, we returned on them. If you hit me, I'm going to hit you.

Films like *Zombie Wars* are fantasmatic attempts to recapture the stage and refigure the residual historic fear of 'pay-back' through its mythical re-inversion. *Zombie Wars*' modern day survivors are the victims, rebels and ultimately victorious – inheritors of colonial fear.

But not all zombie fictional works resolve the anxiety associated with the history of slavery quite so readily. The threat of a future enslavement haunts the genre, fusing past traumatic memory with contemporary anxieties. The earliest zombie films used the figure of the slave as a metonym for western anxieties about industrialisation. In *White Zombie* (1932), zombies labouring in a sugar-cane processing plant assume the monotonous gestures of factory workers creating a metonymic link between enslavement and the industrial working class. *I Walked with a Zombie* (1943) evokes the fear of sexual enslavement shot through with the colonial fear that white women could be sexually enslaved by black masters; *28 Days Later* (2002) and *Zombie Apocalypse* (2010) create apocalyptic scenarios in which women are captured and threatened with sexual enslavement by the new warlords of the future. In *Dawn of the Dead* (1979) enslavement is refigured in the shopping mall with zombie consumers returning to the mall to do the only thing they remember doing – shopping – while, holed up inside the mall, survivors entertain themselves with the only thing left to them, a life of empty consumption. In the 2004 Zack Snyder's remake (*Dawn of the Dead*, 2004), zombies mass at the mall driven 'By memory maybe, instinct', enslaved by the undead drive for endless consumption. In *Land of the Dead* (2005), Romero recreates the zombie/slave as the agent of revolution. Suffering the endless indignity of being shot at, decapitated and butchered by humans, a mutant zombie – empowered with instrumental reason and empathy for fellow zombies – leads an armed insurrection. When his armed zombie horde batters down the walls of Flinders Green – a luxury tower where a new/old white America has reinstalled itself in luxury – they evoke all the peasants, communards and slaves of revolutions past.

Some of the strange semantic associations of zombies today also begin to make sense in the context of this embedded history. To be 'given a zombie' – a distinctly necrophiliac act involving freezing the male genitals in an ice bucket prior to coitus – is, like many other sexual acts classified as zombie, laced with mnemonic traces of cold sexual acts undertaken by force. Sluggish economies, soulless zombie buildings and the catatonia of drugged states all carry the mnemonic trace of an enforced passivity just as economies threatening to collapse, systems falling into chaos and media networks overtaken by viral invasion encrypt the memory of slave revolt.

The collective 'we' of the zombie parade carries this semantic baggage onto the street where, beyond the whimsy and game playing of individuals, it creates a collective manifestation with an incumbent threat. Zombies are the walking wasted rising from the buried memory of history threatening all that *is* with its return. In their mute stumbling shuffles and groans this new public gestures to the crimes of the past as they leer murderously at the future.

Identifying with zombies

But here's the rub. If there is any verity in the argument I've just proposed then why do people take such a great pleasure in *being* zombies? At zombie parades there's a highly charged sense of enjoyment evidently associated with the act of performing *becoming* zombie? Could these joyous revellers be identifying with the mnemonic traces of a traumatic past? Or is there some other promise of pleasure that makes the idea of becoming zombie so evidently joyful?

According to Freud, identification involves a desire to be like another. When we watch a film or read a book we often forge an identification with one or several of the characters in a work of fiction but we tend not to assume their character in its entirety. In identification one identifies with a trait of another, or incorporates an other in the self in order to assume their characteristics. Literature and other fictional realms facilitate identification by creating other worlds and other selves that we can enter into and dwell in. In making fictional lives our own, we expand our experience of other domains, lives, pasts and memories beyond that of our finite individuated existence. Sometimes we forge an identification with the writer behind the text by assuming their words as if they were our own. As Poulet (1969) argues, when we read we play host to an other, the self falls away and *that other's* thoughts, *that other's* affects become our own. Freud (1918) writes that identification – intrinsic to reading and viewing fictional forms – has always created a conduit for people to mediate their relation to death. Literature can provide a way of compensating for the loss of the lives of others and the future loss of the self. Fictional representations of death enable us to identify with the death of a hero or even their murderer and to participate in death without having to die. As Freud (1918: 12) writes, 'We die in identification with a certain hero and yet we outlive her, and quite unharmed, are prepared to die again with the next hero.'

But what if the hero doesn't die? In fact, can't die because they are already dead? Zombies are not heroes. Contemporary zombies are not even human. Their only characteristic is an instinctual hunger – a blood lust. One of the insights of psychoanalysis in relation to identification is that people often identify with the flaws in a character rather than with their strengths, with a disease trait or a symptom. Zombies don't have symptoms, but they are all disease. They are the quintessence of corruption, impurity and decay. When you think about it, it's really quite strange. Zombie marchers manifest a mimetic identification with zombies in their entirety – their dress, gestures, voice and shuffle – but there's nothing to identify with but their violence, their decay and the death that they evoke.

And yet there are few survivors at zombie parades. Those few that turn up clutching cricket bats and imitation swords make a brave show at being human in a zombie world but they lack the *je ne sais quoi* of the zomberati. No gore; no glamour. Ron Scott (2008) documents a similar shift in identificatory patterns amongst gamers, who much to the surprise of manufacturers of computer games prefer to identify with zombies rather than survivors. Battle.net administered by Blizzard Entertainment discovered in their original Tolkien-inspired games that gamers wanted to be orcs more than their noble and heroic counterparts. In response they added a new character 'The Undead' to *Warcraft III*, again assuming few would chose these difficult and unheroic characters. Again, gamers defied their moral expectations. Scott argues that constant feedback led to the eventual complete inclusion of evil characters with full play potential creating a zombie nation, Scott's name for the large community of gamers with zombie avatars.

Of course, survivors offer a rather insecure basis for identification given the way they bleed continuously into the zombie population. Even when they are not ending up as zombies, characters in zombie films are mirrored and doubled by their zombie others. Many critics see this mirroring and doubling of contemporary life and zombies as the motivating cause for the current obsession with zombies but this doesn't really explain why people *identify* with zombies. If there is little difference between zombies and us why would we want to be like them?

The murderer within

As far as I know Freud never wrote anything on zombies, but he can shed some light on the conundrum of what might give zombies their identificatory sticking point. One of the aspects of zombies that mark them out as non-human is their lack of ambivalence. Zombie emotions aren't 'compound', to use

Freud's term, they don't exhibit love and hate towards the same object. Neither do they oscillate between cruelty and pity, or selfishness and altruism. They have a single object and a single drive; hence the representation in many zombie films of media reporting the outbreak of the zombie plague as a virus causing psychopathy. The retarded emotional state of a psychopath is as close in the human world as we can come to a zombie. But zombies aren't psychopaths. They feel no disgust or rage. They don't feel at all; they just hunger. Could this be the trait that zombie fans are identifying with when they dress up as zombies? Could there be a certain pleasure unleashed by the desire to end the difficulty of inhabiting complex compound emotions. After all, being divided in one's feelings is an unpleasant aspect of being human. It certainly makes being in an intimate relationship as vexing as it is pleasurable. This was another of Freud's great insights, albeit one of his 'truths' people least want to hear. Human emotions are ambivalent; love and hatred are fellow travellers, even in our relations to the one object. I think this ambivalence is core to understanding the identificatory appeal of a zombie. Zombies hold out the promise of being unleashed from the social and moral constraints that ambivalence bespeaks. They exhibit a pure and unrestrained aggressive drive, a state that humans en masse only experience in war.

Living through the Great War, Freud noted how war licensed both states and men to overthrow all their moral and ethical precepts. In *Reflections on War and Death* he writes about how war brought to the fore forms of aggression and brutality that prior to the war had been assumed to belong to a more primitive past:

> But the war in which we did not want to believe broke out and brought – disappointment. It is not only bloodier and more destructive than any foregoing war, as a result of the tremendous development of weapons of attack and defence, but it is at least as cruel, bitter, and merciless as

any earlier war. It places itself above all the restrictions pledged in times of peace, the so-called rights of nations, it does not acknowledge the prerogatives of the wounded and of physicians, the distinction between peaceful and fighting members of the population, or the claims of private property. It hurls down in blind rage whatever bars its way, as though there were to be no future and no peace after it is over. It tears asunder all community bonds among the struggling peoples and threatens to leave bitterness, which will make impossible any re-establishment of these ties for a long time to come.

(Freud, 1918: 5)

The 1914–18 war shattered the collective illusion that civilisation's ethical and moral accomplishments signified a decisive end to the barbarities of the past. Unpicking the nature of this disappointment, Freud argues that civilisation can't bring an end to aggression or evil because human character rests on instinctual impulses – neither good nor evil in themselves – which concern the gratification of 'primitive' needs. Impulses such as selfishness and cruelty are rejected by society if they run counter to the needs of the human community – but they don't disappear. Displaced and inhibited, such instincts are diverted to other fields, changing their direction and their object and in some cases turning back on the self. While evil impulses are repressed in individuals and forced to find other channels of expression, states at war give full licence to aggressive impulses. The fundamental human taboo against murder is lifted and human aggression is given full play. In Freud's writing we shouldn't despair at this manifestation of violence because violence is always present; in fact it's intrinsic to the social bond. Civilisation drives these aggressive impulses underground demanding an extraordinarily high renunciation of instinctual impulses and, then, confuses the resultant 'good' behaviour with a radical change in type. War unleashes these bonds sanctifying in the name of patriotism, a return to the pleasure of unrestrained aggression. In war, we are reminded, 'that the past is not simply dead and gone but also, *in potenia* at least, the future' (Weber, 1997: 85).

Freud's pessimistic view of human ethical conduct – as bound by *fear* of the law rather than by achievement of a higher moral state – finds support in zombie visions of a post-apocalyptic future. Survivors in zombie movies do not act well to each other, except within the small bands that demarcate self from other. Men in particular regress, reverting to a hypermasculinity in which patriarchy rules. Men in gangs united under a brutal leader are a mainstay of zombie fiction, appearing as soldiers, as raiders, as looters and as rapists. Fighting it out with gangs of 'good survivors' these future warlords conjure the fantasy of a lived reality that is beyond the law. The apocalypse ends the social order by opening a war-zone between the walking dead and the living in which anything goes, and this includes the moral and ethical behaviour that we think of as intrinsic to character. But, as Freud points out, there is no need to forbid what isn't desired:

> What no human being desires to do does not have to be forbidden, it is self-exclusive. The very emphasis on the commandment; thou shalt not kill, makes it certain that we are descendants from an endlessly long chain of generations of murderers whose love of murder was in their blood as it is perhaps in ours.
> *(Freud, 1918: 15)*

In Freud's vision, we are all murderers, at least in fantasy. Murderous and aggressive desires hitch a ride on more altruistic impulses, hence the double face of human emotion. Egotism can appear as altruism, cruelty as sympathy, love and hate are bound together, especially in our relation to those we love most. As Freud (1918: 5) writes, 'The formation of these reactions is favoured by the fact that many impulses appear almost from the beginning in contrasting pairs; this is the remarkable state of affairs called the ambivalence of feeling.'

This moral conundrum is played out in zombie fictional works where in the absence of law survivors flounder, the more moral characters striving to sustain the law in its absence and the more opportunist taking full possession of the freedom that lawlessness provides. Humans and zombies double each other in zombie texts because the zombie plague unleashes the desire to be zombie in us all. 'We are all infected' as the survivors in *The Walking Dead* discover to their horror.

Guiltless pleasures

In 'Totem and taboo', Freud (2001 [1913]) creates a myth for the genesis of society in which he conceives of the social bond as grounded in bloodshed. In Freud's myth, the brothers, fraught by incestuous desire for the mother, band together to kill the primal father, after which they are overcome by guilt and resurrect the father in the form of a symbolic feast sanctioned by a new law that forbids incest and founds sociality on a brotherhood bound by collective guilt. The point about this myth is not that it describes a historical event but rather that it is a *myth* generated in modernity to give symbolic form to the structural link between violence and law. Murder instantiates society because only a collective act of usurpation can deprive rule by might of its power. Violence also holds open the space of law because it is only by fear and threat that a society can be bound to uphold a law that deprives its members of certain instinctual pleasures. Guilt, Freud argues, is society's way of introverting the performance of pleasurable acts into repressed desires for which we are permanently guilty.

If we compare Freud's myth with the mythical future enacted in zombie scenarios we can see that they reverse the myth inverting its principle elements. In fictional zombie scenarios the zombie plague disbands society. Newly deprived of their humanity, zombies form mass hordes that murder *everyone* and then band together to feast on their flesh in a guiltless and pleasure-filled state. It's a surreal vision in which Freud's myth of social genesis accelerates backwards. The law and its taboos – and the guilt instituted by an original murder – unwind. The symbolic bonds that tie us into community, morality and law are broken and zombies are released into a royal state of licence. The zombie apocalypse opens a war-zone where the power of the state or the sovereign to kill with impunity is generalised to a primal horde unleashed from guilt, from taboo, and from all admonishment. Interestingly, Roget Callois (2001) argues that in modern society only war provides the space of unrivalled transgression that festivals traditionally licensed. Watching zombies at play in zombie festivals one can see the veracity of Freud's (1918) argument that the enjoyment of murder is repressed but never far from our fantasies. Fundamentally beyond the law, zombies unleash the fantasy of the freedom of war where we are licensed to enjoy murder and to feast gloriously on the flesh of others. Zombie festivals create an arena for this fantasy of freedom to be acted out in real space and time. The murderer within – has its moment.

At times, this play invites its participants to come enticingly close to the Real of murder. The 2013 Sydney zombie parade proudly boasts that 'the Sydney Zombie Walk will be invading Maitland Gaol, the gaol that imprisoned Ivan Milat, for two hours of laser tag' (Sydney Zombie Walk, 2013). Milat killed seven young hitchhikers in the Belanglo State Forest in New South Wales between 1989 and 1992. The desire to imitate him proved too much for his great nephews, who recently axed one of their friends to death in the same forest. But imitation is what is on offer at Maitland Gaol. Proximity to Milat promises a special frisson that mere theatricality and military-style weapons cannot provide. It promises proximity to the *Real* of the murderer in a game allowing its players to feel his pleasures – in reach. Such games are proliferating, creating avenues for the zombie nation to move out of the isolation of watching and playing vicariously with murder into collectivised acts of simulated murder. Increasingly, zombie websites offer venues where zombie fans can gather to play at murdering zombies with the maximum semblance of reality. Courses offer real-live-fire anti-zombie training involving point-blank shooting of bleeding zombie targets. Gun manufacturers are raising gun sales through the sale of zombie-themed ammunition and military-style hardware, and websites advise on how to convert weaponry such as shotguns for maximum zombie decapitation potential (The Undead Report, 2012). The only missing detail in this carnival of simulated killing is the promise it holds out — at least in fantasy — of becoming zombie. Raise the red flag! The zombie revolution is coming.

3
ZOMBIE EROTICS

Zombie publics create a third-generation zombie horde quite different from their filmic and textual doubles. When zombies assume the living form of a crowd, the semantic and libidinal elements condensed in the figure of the zombie are re-embodied in a crowd, ritualised in a festival and *rerepresented* in a new form of visual capture that redoubles the mediatised world of zombie. This complicates matters as I discovered when taking photographs of zombies at zombie parades. There's something very distinctive about a photograph. To begin with it is still. It doesn't have the poetic mobility of a film, novel or computer game, nor does it have the living, fluid form of a parade. Photographs snatch a split second out of reality freezing it and giving it duration. Sometime this capture allows us to see things that would go unnoticed.

I imagined that I would take photographs of the zombies at the Adelaide zombie parade and use them in the little book I was writing on zombies, but something happened that made me wonder just what I was doing. In the late afternoon the zombies gathered to picnic, promenade and pose for the dozens of photographers who were shooting at liberty. No 'Please may I?', just a free for all – clicking away as close as you dared – as a zombie on a microphone urged all the photographers to upload their photographs on the Zombie March *Facebook* page as soon as they got home. It was a street photographer's dream. Before the march I had checked with the organisers on whether I needed to register as a photographer but there was no registration system in place and no permission forms. Given the prevalent paranoia about photographers 'taking' unauthorised photographs, this photographic free-for-all seemed part of the long tradition of rule breaking associated with carnival. You can buy a T-shirt on the web that says 'Photography is not a crime', but once I was at home uploading my photographs I found myself in a crime scene of my own making.

It happened when night had fallen and the zombies had moved out of the park to begin the long march across town. Shooting a moaning, gesticulating zombie mass on the move and in the dark is well beyond my technological know-how so I had switched from manual to automatic and begun shooting blind. It was only later that night, as I scanned the images on my computer screen, that I saw her. Those eyes! She'd been moving too fast for my shutter to capture and was little more than an apparition of swirling reds and golden light, but I pared back the colour and there she was. An unquiet image, unsettling, bewildering. A child, twice dressed. Once, in the pink sparkling satin of a fairy costume. Once, blood soaked in the aftermath of horror.

Kids today are familiar with zombies. 'Zombies' is a favourite game at the crèche, and there is a mountain of zombie children's fiction written to provide an imaginary escape from an upsetting reality. But there was something more than fantasy or game playing afoot in this photograph. A 'something more' that transformed the fantasy act of a child dressing up as a figure from a horror-story into a story of horror finding expression through a child.

One thing for certain was that the child was dressed up to be photographed. Zombie parades are a new form of carnival, and like traditional carnival they license the overturning of everyday rules. Cannibalism is the order of the day. People mime the drive to eat each other: tearing, ripping and engorging on the flesh of others, drinking fake blood and moaning for brains. It's not that they're licensed to enjoy violence but *to perform* its enjoyment. It's a performance, a representation of the fictional world of zombie recreated in everyday life in order to create another representation. Zombie marchers become zombies on websites enabling their participants to enter into, and become part of, the endlessly proliferating network of virtual images and texts that feed the proliferating hunger for ever more zombie images and texts. This is why photographers get open slather at zombie parades. They are conduits, enabling the pantomime of ordinary people to cross over into the hyper-reality of virtual representation. They turn people dressed-up as zombies … into zombies.

Photographs of zombies at zombie parades have an added effect: they transform the transient moments of a zombie parade into an event with duration giving continuity to an otherwise discontinuous event. Circulating in suspended animation on the web, photographs of zombies at zombie parades reference and double cinematic zombies. As photographs in global circulation they enter into this generic tradition, fusing with zombie as a fictional form with its own specific longevity and duration.

The French semiotician Roland Barthes (1980) suggests that photographs also have their own specific kind of contingency in the way they arrest objects and subjects in time. Photographs, he argues, snare something, or someone, in a singular moment of passing time in a fixed form. The photograph captures a *this* that is irrecoverable and yet is demonstrably present in the ephemeral container of the photograph. This is why photographs are evocative of death, he argues, because they become the referent of their own lost moment. As Barthes (1980: 13) writes, 'Photography transforms subject into object, and even, one might say, into a museum object', because photography dispossesses the living, creating an objectal realm in which 'this' becomes an object that once was and is no longer. Moreover, unlike other forms of representation, the photograph is a sign that appears to be indissoluble from its referent; it cleaves to what it signifies as if photography itself is not a sign system but a purely transparent representation of something or someone that once was. This is why photographs – at least for people unfamiliar with the reality altering potential of lenses, apertures and shutter speeds – appear to capture a reality undiluted by representation.

But the object represented in a zombie photograph is not just something or someone that once was. Zombie photographs capture a person theatricalising a zombie, a thing that belongs on a movie screen – pretending to be a thing that once was. As a representation, the zombie's referent is always deferred – even in 'reality' a zombie refers to something else. This deferred referentiality is intrinsic to the fictional construction of zombies as a container emptied of former subjectivity and filled with a new kind of animus. A photograph of a zombie marries this deferred reference with the doubling of presence and absence played out through the figure of death. Death is foregrounded in the presentation of a corpse and yet remains displaced by its animation. This means photographs of zombies are playing a fairly complex game with representation – and with death.

The subject matter of these photographs – people pretending to be fictional dead things that have reanimated – changes the evocation of death that Barthes argues is specific to photography. For Barthes, the photograph captures the singularity of a time, of a life and (with time) a death, and then confers a death-like status to a singular life or moment. But zombies are the very antithesis of singular existence. To pretend to be a zombie is to theatricalise non-being. With very few exceptions,[1] fictional zombies in text and on screen are devoid of character, even if they are dressed up as the characters of fiction's past. The zombie is an everyman who has become a no man. Even if it was 'one of us' before its death, zombification cancels out prior subjectivity. The zombie is a depersonalised dead thing that by virtue of the suspended form of its death is stripped of all subjectivity. Zombies are a new kind of thing – the subjectless dead. The only human trait left to the zombie is an instinctual hunger manifesting in a distinctly non-human form because zombie instincts are without ambivalence. Unlike humans, whose destructive impulses are usually rhymed with opposing drives, zombies are only hungry and they hunger for only one thing – life.

In this sense, zombies are not the dead. Unlike zombies, the dead generally stay dead, and they belong to us. Whatever difficult relations we may have with the dead, these relations are marked by human forms of possession. Through ceremony, ritual and belief system, human cultures sustain a hold on the dead. Albeit separate from the human world, the dead are susceptible to the representative matrix of their human provenance. Even the dead of centuries past can be reclaimed by historical memory, imagination and myth-making, hence the oft-quoted lines, 'death ends a life, not a relationship' (Albom, 1997: 174).

Inter-subjective relations between the living and the zombified are another matter. Zombies are not dead but they represent death unleashed from all human bonds. Unlike the dead, this death is radically asocial. The fundamental human taboo, 'Thou shalt not kill', is meaningless to zombies. When zombies kill the living they are not violating a human taboo but signifying a radical otherness to humanity. Insentient and mute, with neither life nor meaning, zombies press upon the tenuous and fragile spaces, not just of the social order but also of life itself. They incarnate a vision of death as an ever-present putrefying morass, a death that seeks only to reassume that which it has lent life. As photographs or moving images, zombies do not evoke death as we know it, but incarnate death *as we wish to forget it*. They give continuity in visual and verbal form to a death that representation would foreclose. Death loses its individuation, its face. The death that shadows photography – of singular lives and singular moments – is overtaken by the death we most fear and can least comprehend. Mass death, death that sweeps us all in its path leaving us faceless, unknown, unmarked, unremembered. Zombies give this life-devouring, a-human death a contemporary *face*. When zombie fans seek immortality in the virtual world of images circling globally on the web, they lend their faces to this non-human death sweeping all in its path.

Mixed-up messages

Little wonder, then, that my camera caught me out unawares, capturing in a photograph the underbelly of the game zombies – and their photographers – play with death. When I look at this photo of a child in a blood-spattered fairy dress I see a little girl playing dress-up with the latest scary craze. But something else animates the scene and it's not just the overt visual shock of seeing a young girl covered in blood and pretending to be a dead thing. The girl looks bewildered, violated. Perhaps her eyes are registering the shock that someone, *the One*, poured blood over her pretty dress. Or perhaps she just has the eyes of a brutalised child. I'll never know. Roland Barthes (1980) calls this the *punctum*, a second element in a photograph – a sting, a speck, a mark or a wound that cuts a hole in a photographic image overturning its civility. For Barthes, this is an element in the image itself, but looking at the photograph I become aware of an other uncivil presence *outside* the picture's frame. An *other* that looks hungrily at the image I have conjured of a violated girl.

The girl's eyes put me in mind of George Bataille's (1986 [1957]: 11) evocation of the Marquis de Sade, 'There is not a libertine some little way gone in vice, who does not know what a hold murder has on the senses.'

Through dint of my technological incompetence and the camera's technical wizardry, I had created an erotic fantasy of a particularly perverse kind. Or had I? The street had given me this image. It had come from the *Real*. The camera had captured something present on that street – the sinister, erotic underside of zombie. The girl, who was not a character in a film or narrative, had nevertheless been 'taken' by a recording mechanism and transformed into a representation. She had become fixed in the lifelessness of a photograph: a girl on the threshold of death, bloodied, brutalised but not dead yet. From active participant as a zombie in a pantomime she had become a victim – not of the monsters found in horror movies, but of another kind of monstrous gaze at loose in the world. What would feminist film theory make of this? Monster and victim; active and passive; her pleasure his pleasure – they were 'all mixed up' (*Night of the Living Dead*, 1968).

A few days before the zombie parade a young woman was abducted from an inner city suburb of Melbourne. The woman was raped and murdered, just one of a string of murders in these streets in recent years. Thousands of people marched silently to protest this brutal end to a life and hundreds of people left flowers on the street. The murdered woman had been abducted from the street where my daughters and I had shopped and dined and socialised for several years. Murder in a community cuts close, even if you've never met the victim or the family involved. It's a fragilising affair that leaves you shuddering deeply in the empty moments of the day and endlessly repeating that parental act of mentally checking on the children, long after they have grown. But here I was, just a few days later, walking alongside thousands of people playing dress-up with murder, and I was having fun. So was my daughter, who was shuffling along beside me, making up for her relatively demure zombie costume by extra-loud expository calls for brains. Evidently we were all participating in the kind of disassociation that fantasy allows. Or were we? The photograph of the girl

FIGURE 3.1 Family feast, zombie parade, Adelaide, October 2012.

suggested that there might be something else in play besides the pleasurable identification we were partaking in – in fantasy. Like the pleasurable acts of murder happening in streets not far from where we played, zombie games eroticise death.

The erotics of death

The writing of French philosopher Georges Bataille (1986 [1957]) can shed some light here. Bataille's understanding of culture is violent often to the point of celebration and suffers from an infatuation with violent sexual and religious rites. De Sade is his touchstone and, while he distances himself from de Sade's more excessive acts, he remains compelled by the power of his erotic world. Bataille's writing is also often coloured by an unconscious triumphalism in regard to masculine sexual violence. Despite this – or perhaps because of it – his writing is particularly relevant for understanding the eroticised violence of zombie cultural forms.

Death will always have an erotic component according to Bataille (1986) because the function of erotism is to break down the taboos, patterns and rules that sustain individuals in a rule-bound social order. Eroticism, played out in physical acts of violence, in sexual acts and in religious rituals, creates a conduit for individuated subjects to experience the asocial collective state of death without succumbing to it.

Bataille (1986) understands humans as profoundly ambivalent towards their species being as individuated subjects, bound by their nature to live isolated, individual and finite lives. Death has an erotic component, he argues, because sex and death frame individuation. Sexual reproduction determines our existence as individuated beings, and as such makes us subject to death. Bataille conceptualises individuation existentially, rather than sociologically, within these polarities of birth and death:

> Each being is distinct from all others. His birth, his death, the events of his life may have an interest for others but he alone is directly concerned in them. He is born alone. He dies alone. Between one being and another, there is a gulf, a discontinuity.
>
> *(Bataille, 1986 [1957]: 12)*

At times almost oneiric in his visual intensity, Bataille (1986) erects a view of culture as a flimsy fortification held erect only by culturally universal taboos which carve out a tenuous zone for the work of society. Taboos against innate violent and sexual drives sustain the space of society through the creation of a law-bound state, but they also incite transgression which he conceives as the principle means for humans to experience the continuity of life that our discontinuity separates us from. The fundamental taboos against murder, against the eating of human flesh and against sexual acts outside of prescribed limits, create a zone freed from the dominion of death and the violence of reproduction. But taboos are laws that are made to be violated.

Humans need transgression in order to draw close to the violent excesses of the realms of death and reproduction. Through transgression we are freed momentarily to dwell in an animal existence outside the control of social law.

In his account, humans are both fascinated and horrified by death. They desire its promise of a reprieve from the isolation of individuation – death promises a return to continuity – and yet they fear the transition it augurs from living sentience into putrid decay. The nausea that accompanies the thought of the putrescence of death is married with erotic fascination. Death disgusts and death compels. Through death, we are torn violently from discontinuity into continuity:

> The most violent thing of all for us is death which jerks us out of a tenacious obsession with the lastingness of our discontinuous being. We blench at the thought that the separate individuality within us must suddenly be snuffed out.
> *(Bataille, 1986 [1957]: 16)*

Death carries this threat of violence, hence the great disquiet that death evokes, and yet being human – being isolated and individuated – carries its own form of anguish. Eroticism unfolds in this violent domain of transition between life and death, between individuated isolation and the continuity of death. Bataille conceives of death as more *Real* than life itself. It is the ferment of life, explosive, generative and devouring; all individuated life finds its destiny in its cycle of endless renewal. And all cultures play on this boundary creating highly eroticised rituals and practices as transports into a death that is both desired and feared. Ideally such rituals go to the edge of death but no further, although in the case of human sacrifice an individual death creates a collective space of revelation:

> In sacrifice, the victim is divested not only of clothes but of life (or is destroyed in some way if it is an inanimate

object). The victim dies and the spectators share in what his death reveals. This is what religious historians call the element of sacredness. This sacredness is the revelation of continuity through the death of a discontinuous being to those who watch it as a solemn rite. A violent death disrupts the creature's discontinuity; what remains, what the tense onlookers experience in the succeeding silence, is the continuity of all existence with which the victim is now one.

(Bataille, 1986 [1957]: 22)

Blurring the distinction between sacrifice, sexual penetration and murder, Bataille (1986 [1957]: 123) argues that these three forms of Eros participate in the same drive to touch the edge of death by violent transgression. Eroticism, in this sense, 'is assenting to life up to the point of death'. Sexuality carries the same inner meaning of violence because it violates the very being of its practitioners translating them into a state bordering on death, presupposing a partial dissolution of the person, as s/he exists in a state of discontinuity:

> The lover strips the beloved of her identity no less than the blood-stained priest his human or animal victim. The woman in the hands of her assailant is despoiled of her being. With her modesty she loses the firm barrier that once separated her from others and made her impenetrable. She is brusquely laid open to the violence of the sexual urges set loose in the organs of reproduction; she is laid open to the impersonal violence that overwhelms her from without.
>
> *(Bataille, 1986 [1957]: 90)*

A dissolution, a fusing, an intermingling – for Bataille (1986 [1957]: 17), 'the whole business of eroticism is to destroy the self-contained character of the participators as they are in their normal lives'. He links stripping naked to this idea of dissolution, as if nakedness is in stark contrast to discontinuous existence: 'It is a state of being beyond the confines of the self. Bodies open out to a state of continuity through secret channels that give us a feeling of obscenity' (Bataille, 1986 [1957]: 17).

But how much more obscene is the opening out of the body in the zombie feast? The zombie horde doesn't just open out the body: it devours it. In fact, zombies do what some men imagine doing in the act of sexual penetration and others fear being done to them. They dissolve selfhood through the act of possession. Zombie eroticism involves a long striptease of the body as it is violently laid open to the hands and mouths of an anonymous horde. In the zombie feast the body is stripped not only of its clothes but also of its skin. Obscenely opened to the gaze, the subject of a zombie feast is the ultimate visual metaphor for loss of self-possession. The body is opened to the gaze, its interior cavities displayed in the full ripeness of its life, as the horde literally enters into and consumes the living body. Classically the subject of the feast is also its observer, watching in horror as its 'self' is opened up, eviscerated and parcelled out. A consummation of the one by the many, the feast is both sexual and sacrificial. A moment when 'we' – the viewers, the survivors, the victim – watch the devouring of particularity as one becomes the many. Outside all social law, this feasting on the living – graphically portrayed in the most excessive moments of cinematic history – creates an eroticised zone of violent fascination. The zombie feast condenses death, reincarnation, the consumption of human flesh and the erotically charged realm of the body in its most naked and viscid states.

Street sex

So what had my camera recorded? The image of the girl was certainly incendiary. If I had put it up on the web as the organisers of the parade urged me to do, I would have given its erotic invitation duration. It would have turned a moment of street theatre into a super-heated evocation of a young girl, bloodied and brutalised gesturing towards death, and play-acting murder. A girl, moreover, who was pretending to be dead, inviting the viewer into a game in which the passage into, and beyond death, was a zone of play.

So what was *in play* in the street theatre of the zombie parade? The answer to this question *might* be that participating in the theatrical pageantry of a zombie parade – like watching zombie films on screen – has little to do with violent acts. Nobody is hurt in a zombie parade just as neither zombies nor survivors are injured in the violent altercations depicted on screen. These are fictional scenarios at a far distance from real acts of violence. When zombies rip bodies to pieces in zombie movies and feast on entrails, the creators of these scenarios are not licensing violence any more than organisers of zombie marches are encouraging zombie walkers to devour their onlookers. Fiction and theatre are not reality, nor is it their function to represent standardised codes of behaviour or sanitised moral, social or political worlds. Fiction serves other needs; it opens spaces of freedom to imagine all possible futures, all possible scenarios. But the young girl I photographed was neither a fictional entity nor a zombie. She was real and yet, at the same time, she had become a new kind of *thing*. Snared in the ephemeral form of a photograph she had become an erotic surface on which a violent imaginary could play out its games. As if the plagues of the past had returned, she and all her fellow monsters wending their way across all the major cities of the world were hard at play, creating a new St Vitus dance to give erotic form to death – inviting us all into its pageantry, its play and its *real*. My camera, in the manner of cameras, had given her *thing* perpetuity but the fantasy she had been hooked into was a photograph awaiting a camera.

4
THE ZOMBIE OPERA

Still puzzling over the photograph of the blood-spattered girl in a fairy dress, I'm struck by how different its erotic language is to the poetic language of the first modern zombie incarnation, Romero's *Night of the Living Dead* (1968). There are young zombified girls aplenty in this film – stumbling through the night and plucking at the flesh of the newly dead – but the film's language doesn't lend itself to this kind of violent erotic fantasy. The language of the zombie feast – of blood, ruptures, tears and entrails – is the same, but there is nothing eroticised about its violence. Quite the reverse. In Romero's first zombie film attention keeps shifting from oneiric scenes of zombies gathering and eating to the captivating drama unfolding in a besieged farmhouse. The zombies massing outside interrupt and frame the drama but they never colonise our, the viewers', point of view, which is always moving between these two very different realities and their intermittent violent intersection. This juxtaposition of the zombie crowd and the individuated narrative of the survivors creates its own poetics: a grammatical structure underpinning the film's allegorical eloquence. The power of Romero's original film as a critical exploration of modern violence – rather than a celebration of it – has to do with the dialectic he establishes between the mute violence of the zombie mass and the individuated narratives of the survivors.

The enigma of the zombies can only be grasped within this dialectic. On their own, zombies don't signify much at all, but embedded within the dialectic of individuation and massification they assume an immense allegorical power. Of course many fictional zombie works are simply celebrations of an eroticised violence. *Redneck Zombies* (1989), for example, is one of many such films whose entire *raison d'être* is to visualise ever new forms of dissection, decomposition and decay for the spectator's pleasure. *Zomblies* (2010) exists purely to showcase special effects, actions scenes and some powerful weaponry. There are many zombie fictional works like this, endlessly repeating mute and repetitive dissections of bodies. Some argue that the graphic montages of extreme violence typical of zombie films have a radically decentring power deriving from the way they dismember bodies, texts and the affective responses of their viewers (Arnzen, 1994). But Zombie texts, however extreme their violence, can be the stupidest of works or the sharpest, just as zombie publics can be mindlessly violent or exuberantly creative. Violent montage, however fragmentary explosive or uncanny, can't in itself explain the allegorical power of zombies today. Zombies, at their best, do more than explode our 'viewing positions' and at their worst this is all they do.

Part of what zombies do – their theatrical function within the genre – is provide a chorus, a de-individuated mass framing and contextualising the actions of individuated protagonists. The crowd – so often idealised in the ideologies of the twentieth century – is revisioned as a mute and brutal mass animated by a singular impulse, a will to devour the living. The moan-filled cries of the zombie chorus – susurrating with the death rattle, hungering to devour life – frame the messy, confused and often treacherous acts of individuated survivors. In zombie films, the individual carries the spark of life; en masse there are only zombies. But, en masse, zombies are always getting the better of the living. One by one, survivors slip up and transform in a passage of seconds, from individual subject to viscera feeding the dumb hunger of the crowd. The camera (and zombie fans) love these moments when hundreds of hands and mouths, tear and rip in rhythmic unison. But for people who hate zombie films it's the evident *jouissance* on display in these moments that disgusts them. Zombie films seem to invite their viewers into an unmediated enjoyment of violence, horror spilling into the pleasure of watching living bodies mutate into a mess of entrails. Reviewers often reinforce this by gauging the success of a zombie film by its capacity to deliver new scenes of graphic butchery, creating a discourse in which 'uncompromised' graphic violence becomes an aesthetic virtue in itself. Critical writing on the other hand tends to interpret these scenes of violence allegorically. Steven Shaviro (1993: 4), for example, argues that zombies are a:

> nearly perfect allegory for the inner logic of capitalism, whether this be taken in the sense of the inner exploitation of living labour by dead labour, the death-like regimentation of factories and other social spaces, or the artificial externally driven stimulation of consumers.

Thinking about this – and after many nights watching zombie films – what strikes me is that attempts to define the meaning of the allegory confuse figurative language with indexical language. Zombies aren't medieval allegories; they don't have a closed indexical field of reference. They are intrinsically modern figures slipping freely across the semantic field fusing and forging new figurations with the dynamism of modernity itself. This doesn't mean that zombies don't also carry metaphorical baggage with them; evidently they do, as we've seen with the confused, contradictory and often *inverted* desires they evoke in relation to slavery. But zombies are poetic as well as historical and social figures, and understanding the way they function allegorically requires being attentive to this. Whatever social reach they may have as figures of the systemic violence of capitalism, or of commodity relations in late modernity, this takes effect through the poetic structures that give them their meaning.

Through lines

Romero's immediate inspiration was Richard Matheson's 1954 vampire novel *I am Legend* (Matheson, 2004 [1954]), which, as Gregory A. Waller argues, dispensed with the long tradition of vampires as seductive, aristocratic and masterful, making a new form of monster en masse, an undifferentiated mass monster no longer defined by its individual characteristics:

> In *I am Legend* there is no seductive, aristocratic Dracula, no wish-fulfilling Barlow, no King-Vampire at all, just the mindless undead, who 'walked and walked about on restless feet, circling each other like wolves, never looking at each other once'.
>
> *(Waller, 1986: 256)*

According to Romero it was the 'socio-political through line' of *I am Legend* that inspired him initially into writing a story about a revolutionary society coming into being – as a zombie society (Yakir, 1977). Neville, the protagonist of Matheson's novel – the sole human in a post-human world – comes to the painful realisation that he is the chancre in the way of the success of a new vampiric society. His singularity as the sole individual human standing against the monster horde is reframed by the end of the film into that of a counter-revolutionary blocking the path to the new (Christie, 2011). In *I am Legend*, the vampires are the future and the human becomes their monstrous past. Romero borrows from Matheson's inversion of the heroic individual into a mass monster to create a filmic structure, in which the individual and the mass mirror and double the monstrosity of each other. The critical acuity of *Night of the Living Dead* has to do with this refusal to make the monster the site of a projected and externalised horror. Instead, Romero socialises monstrosity. Zombies, like all moderns, belong in crowds, those latter-day inventions of modern cities. A zombie is always a mass event; a chance encounter with a zombie multiplies with the regularity of massproduction. One becomes the many.

Violence individuated

The first modern zombies in *Night of the Living Dead* are rather quizzical creatures. They munch on the bones of the living much as an animal might chew contentedly on the limbs of its prey. Body bits in this first modern zombie film have none of the technicolour splendour of later zombie spectacles, nor are they opened up with the frenzied excesses of later films. In *Night of the Living Dead*, body parts look much like the meat we might feed a dog. The camera focuses on joints of meat rather than disembowelled entrails and on the act of feeding rather than the frenzy of evisceration. These zombies hardly function as allegories of the systemic violence of capitalism or of mass consumption – in fact they eat rather demurely – except in the sense that they are intrinsically allegorical as bodies inexplicably animating death and encroaching on life. Later films by Romero lend themselves to such reading but at least at the moment of its genesis, violence in the modern zombie genre is both more local and more *literal*.

In *Night of the Living Dead* Romero juxtaposes this strange bestial crowd with seven entrapped survivors struggling to become a group able to withstand the death on their doorstep. Within the limited economy of a farmhouse – defended by a single gun and some planks and nails – the seven survivors manage, within a single night, to form factions and rivalries, and to enter into competition for control and power. Familial relations amongst the survivors are no less rivalrous and claustrophobic. The film begins with brother and sister Barbara and Johnnie enacting the tired ritual of commemorating the death of a father they barely remember. This ambivalence extends to each other, and leads ultimately to their zombification. There is little love lost between Helen and Harry Cooper. When their daughter Hannah kills her mother with a trowel and chews on her dead father's arm, there is almost a sense of relief that the repressed violence of familial relations has finally been aired. The relationship between the young couple, Judy and Tom, is less ambivalent, but they still end up causing each other's death. Only Ben, the film's sole black protagonist, displays the virtues of a hero. He is rational, resourceful, courageous and solicitous of the near-catatonic Barbara, but his attempts to lead and defend the group are thwarted by Harry, who is unremittingly self-interested, belligerent and cowardly. This could make for a morality play except that by the end of the film the distance between the two men has closed. When Ben criticises Harry's failure to respond to Barbara's cries for help, Harry ripostes: 'I'm not going to take that kind of chance when we got a safe-place and you're telling us we got to risk our lives … just because somebody needs help.' But as the drama plays out Ben's moral authority collapses as we watch him blithely smoking as he listens to the radio compère's announcement of the atrocities occurring all around, and then observe him shoot a disarmed and disgraced Harry – in cold blood. What emerges from this night of the living dead is less the exceptional violence of the zombies than the subterranean normalcy of violence. The humans, like the zombies, are *casually* violent. Under siege, the innate violence of the survivors has emerged and merged with that of the zombies. By punctuating individuated acts of violence with that of the zombie crowd, Romero creates a drama in which the mass violence of the chorus becomes individuated as each member of the group emerges as its *vector*. And by the end of the film each individuated subject has slipped up and become one – of them.

Ben survives the night of the living dead only to be mistaken for a zombie and shot by the National Guard. The quiet acts of murder by bestial zombies take on a new hue as we see him transformed into a piece of meat hauled around by the meat-hooks of the all-white militia. Shot as a sequence of grainy black and white photographs this final scene departs from the theatricality of the farmhouse set to reframe its mini-drama of inter-group violence within the long history of race relations. As the credits roll, we see: the legs of booted men, meat hooks in hand, standing over the dead body of Ben; meat hooks wielded by white hands dragging the body like a piece of meat in an abattoir; and Ben's body being tossed on the pile of burning zombies like a piece of refuse. All the film's references to bestiality are gathered up and realised in this horrific moment when the absurdity of the film's premise takes on the reality of the long history of colonialism, slavery and racial oppression. It's clear at least in this inaugural film that the violence of the zombie chorus is doing more than inviting us to enjoy the spectacle of the body dismembered, nor do they function to destabilise or decentre our viewing positions. This film keeps its viewers critically alert from start to finish. Constantly juxtaposing the casual inadvertent violence of the zombie crowd and the individuated willed violence of survivors, the film creates an abstracted after-effect of violence which Romero then grounds shockingly, within a specific group and a specific history. Through the use of the crowd as a chorus he frames and illuminates the inner violence of individuated stories and then uses these individuated stories to evoke mass violence. Violence is individuated and en masse, abstracted and historically concrete. It's not simply that zombies are us but rather that the beast in the zombie speaks of 'us' and our history. And 'we' in this sense are again 'all mixed up', individuated and en masse, zombie and survivor, victim and perpetrator, coloniser and colonised.

The opera of Hiroshima

Speaking about making the film, Romero says, 'I love the Godzilla films. They're not scary at all, but as a phenomenon born out of the war, the bomb, they say more to me than *Hiroshima, Mon Amour* (cited in Yakir, 1977: 2). But once Romero mentions *Hiroshima Mon Amour* (1959) it's hard to think about the two films in isolation. On first take they seem at a far remove. *Hiroshima Mon Amour* is a distinguished and celebrated work of classic modernist cinema created by two famous artists of the twentieth century, Alain Resnais and Margeurite Duras. *Night of the Living Dead* is a work of pop art that began life as a B-grade movie shot cheaply by a group of young American advertisers who wanted to move into making features. One work stands in cinematic history for its creation of a new relation to the poetic representation of traumatic reality, the other as the founding text in a new genre of Hollywood horror, a genre that created a new hyper-realism in the visual representation of the dismemberment of the human body. The genre born out of Romero's *Night of the Living Dead* has little of the subtle poetics of Duras and Resnais's film. Zombie films create a carnival of horror, a parade of cadavers stripteasing their insides and they don't mince words – just bodies. If the best zombie films approach the high art status of a work like *Hiroshima Mon Amour*, they do so through very different logics. But, when we look at these films together, what emerges is that they share a formal quality. Both films attempt to create a poetics able to realise an encounter with the raw violence of modernity through the use of the crowd as a chorus to frame and illuminate the inner violence of individuated stories, and then uses these individuated stories to evoke violence beyond its representation. In both works violence is individuated and en masse, abstracted and historically concrete.

In the stage notes to *Hiroshima Mon Amour*, Marguerite Duras uses the term 'operatic' to describe the exchange that unfolds in the opening sequences of the film she and Alain Resnais co-created as a work intended to make this 'horror [of Hiroshima] rise again from its ashes' (Duras, 1961: 9). Operatic is a strange term to use in the context, particularly as she follows it up with the phrase '*the Opera of Hiroshima*' (italics original, Duras, 1961: 10). For Duras, the event of Hiroshima lends itself to thinking through the allegory of opera, an idea that many might find – at least in the first instance – obscene. The deep hush that follows intense suffering would seem to be the very antithesis of operatic excess. It's not difficult, however, to imagine this same phrase being used to describe a contemporary zombie film – a librettist could have a lot of fun with a zombie chorus. To understand what Duras means by her rather obscure phrase we need to backtrack to the questions confronting artists and intellectuals in the aftermath of the Second World War.

By the end of the war a saturation point had been reached – not in the art of killing but in the belief that knowledge or art could chart a path out of destruction. In *Regarding the Pain of Others* American cultural critic Susan Sontag (2003) argues that between the First and Second World Wars there was a commonly shared belief that representation could empower change. In that period, with governments declaring an end to war as a way of implementing national policy, there was a widespread belief that war could be stopped and a determination to ensure that the horrors of the First World War would never be repeated (Sontag, 2003). Sontag argues that running through all the post-First World War intellectual, literary and artistic denunciations of war is the assumption that all good people, faced with the horrors of war (through the shock of seeing images of war, for example), would unite in its denunciation. Sontag (2003: 14–15) illustrates her argument with Ernst Friedrich's (1987 [1924]) book of photography, *Krieg dem Kriege!* (*War Against War*):

> This is photography as shock therapy: an album of more than one hundred and eighty photographs mostly drawn

> from German military and medical archives ... the reader has an excruciating tour of forty years of ruin, slaughter and degradation: pages of wrecked and plundered churches and castles, obliterated villages, ravaged forests, torpedoed passenger steamers, shattered vehicles, hanged conscientious objectors, half naked prostitutes in military brothels, soldiers in death agonies after a poison gas attack, skeletal Armenian children. Almost all the sequences in *War Against War* are difficult to look at. ... but surely the most unbearable pages in this book, the whole of which was designed to horrify and demoralise, are in the section entitled 'The Face of War', twenty-four close-ups of soldiers with huge facial wounds.

The work was acclaimed by writers, artists and intellectuals who believed the book would have a decisive influence on public opinion, but as Sontag (2003) points out, by 1930 *War Against War* had gone through ten editions in Germany and had been translated into many languages. But the war came anyway.

Created in the aftermath of the Second World War, *Hiroshima Mon Amour* reflects a far more pessimistic understanding of human pathology and of the limited power of representation to either represent horror or to limit its passage into the world. Duras and Resnais hold no belief in the power of graphic representation to bring an end to violence. Instead, they attempt to create a work of horror that in Duras's terms has done away with 'the description of horror by means of horror' (Duras, 1961: 9). In *Hiroshima Mon Amour,* Duras strives to arrive at an indescribable reality that is *beyond representation*. She called this notion of writing, 'the approach of the inner shadow where the archives of the self are to be found' (cited in Adler, 2000: 193).

The film opens with two bodies making love, their entangled limbs melding and separating. We don't see their faces, only their limbs. Until the end of the film, these two characters remain nameless. We meet them in the first instance only as body parts, mutilated by the camera that dissects them. They are strangely etiolated, glistening with what might be water or ash, or perhaps melted skin fused with ash. They could be bodies either in the act of love or death, their violent spasms that of love or death. We hear their voices speaking of Hiroshima. 'He: "You saw nothing in Hiroshima. Nothing." She: "I saw everything. Everything."' (*Hiroshima Mon Amour*, 1959). Their voices are syncopated with a musical score that creates a rhythmic intensity. As Frédérick de Towarnicki writes: 'to begin with the highly pitched tone was disorienting, then it became an astonishing score where the dialogue was transformed into melodic lines that projected a kind of lyrical and cadenced matter on to the screen' (cited in Adler, 2000: 225). As they speak, the camera moves from these two merging bodies into a volley of images of the aftermath of Hiroshima. The viewer sees the Hiroshima museums and reconstructions of the bomb and its aftermath: the exhibits of the material traces left from the bomb, the melted bicycles and bottle tops, the shattered stone, the remnants of charred bone and fallen hair, the photos and film footage of the survivors in the immediate aftermath of the apocalyptic event.

It is only after this long introductory sequence that the two characters individuate into a French woman and a Japanese man. The film follows the course of their chance encounter, a brief amorous affair that has no history or future. Two individuals meet in a bar, are drawn to each other and make love in a liaison that cannot possibly lead anywhere. They are just two of the strangers that mass society brings together. Duras calls them a chance couple: one of the 'chance meetings that occur everywhere in the world' (Duras, 1961: 8). This chance couple merge with the crowd and then reindividuate in a Dionysian/ Apollonian waltz in which they are never simply themselves but always the indices of a mass reality. Resnais stages them again and again in crowd scenes, which punctuate and frame their singular drama.

Intrinsic to the horror of this film is that love enters into the story only as a delusion. The woman desires the man because of the inevitable death of their affair; its impossibility allows her to re-experience the feelings associated with the death of her German lover in the final days of the war. What this new stranger does for her is invade her body with the emotional stench of death. He allows her to re-enter the memory of the time when she mourned her dead lover trapped within a cellar and to return to the moment when her body fused with his dead body lying beneath her. As the film unfolds we come to understand that whatever passes as intimacy between them is just a ruse to enable each of them to pursue their singular paths into the violent past. What they both effectively desire in each other is the recollection of a death, of a loss that neither can countenance except through its repetition. Oscillating between the individuated stories of the lovers drawn from the violence of war, and the disaggregated, de-individuated crowd scenes the film arrives at a poetic evocation of horror that is both intimate, elided and ever-present. Horror emerges beyond representation, beyond the actual words and images used, out of the revelation of an intimate torment (the horror of loving only in order to inhabit death) that bespeaks the manifold horrors of millions of other stories all inhabited intimately and unspeakably by the anonymous crowd.

Romero's poetics of horror couldn't be more different in its explicit representation of graphic depictions of the horror of war, but Romero seems to have learned a poetic lesson from Duras and Resnais – an operatic lesson. *Hiroshima Mon Amour* not only unfolds in time but also keeps time like a work of music, punctuating its individuated acts with the chorus of the crowd to which, and from which, the individuals emerge and return. Made a decade after *Hiroshima Mon Amour*, *Night of the Living Dead* shares Duras and Resnais's awareness of the limited power of representation to mediate the violence of modernity. Both films contend with the sheer numerical violence of death in the twentieth century: seventy million by the century's end – dead in war. This statistic makes the question of the individual's death, the suffering and loss that surrounds a single loved person, almost an obscene preoccupation given its repetition *ad nauseum* across all the cultures and countries of the world. The one is always an indices of the millions. But while Duras's aesthetic response to this is to try and open up a space beyond representation using the intimate horror of a single story to illuminate the horror of mass death, Romero creates a new visual spectacle of mass death moving inexorably into possession of individuated lives. Rather than hollowing out representation he fills it in with the stench of the cadaver, with the body in all its lurid states of decomposition and animated with the violence of history. The walking dead – both victim and perpetrator – signpost the precariousness of each singular life, even as it moves en masse to devour it. What Romero learns from Duras and Resnais is how to use the opposition between the crowd and individuated narratives to create an operatic movement between chorus and characters playing out in time and sounding time – as each life falls into death. Later zombie films rarely achieve the aesthetic economy of *Night of the Living Dead*, nor its political acuity – but they all bear the traces of this poetic structure.

The sacrificial scene at the centre of *La Horde* (2010), an aptly named French zombie-gangster movie, exemplifies this. *La Horde* stages a brutal encounter with a bunch of gangsters and cops on the night of the zombie apocalypse. An unrelentingly mediocre film, there is one high point – the death scene of the chief cop. Ouessem has been bitten, making his zombification inevitable, but still on the side of the humans he sacrifices his last human moments, taking on the zombie horde to buy time for the remaining three survivors. There is nothing attractive about these survivors. Just prior to this sacrificial scene the viewer has observed one of the survivors, gangster chief Markudi, beat a zombified former gangster to pulp as he shouts 'I'm a Nigerian' – a *non sequitur* that at a stretch might signify a troubled past of communal tensions and ethnic strife but really doesn't signify much at all. The other two survivors are René, an inhabitant of the decrepit apartment building they are trapped in and a former veteran of the indo-China war. He refers to zombies as 'chinks' and makes laughing matter of his dead wife's fallen bosom. And Aurore, a female cop who makes René look sensitive. The film's sub-text is minimal. At most it makes a feeble attempt to paint these repellent characters of the French ghetto as zombified *avant la letter*. In this context, Ouessem's sacrifice unfolds in a space of almost zero affective resonance; he's going to end up zombified but we don't much like him, and we don't much care. But as the attenuated scene of his transition into zombie unfolds he comes to personify the *principium individuationis*, looming out from the monster horde in a heroic insistence – even as his entrails are passing from hand to mouth – of his being *One*. Running into the zombie horde like a rugby hooker he knocks zombies flying, shooting unceasingly – he is one human against thousands of zombies. Finally, on top of a car and encircled by a crowd of heads and clutching hands, he takes to them with a machete, lopping at the inexhaustible supply of heads and limbs. The cacophony of moans, the rhythmic clutching and clawing of hands, the repetitive spurts of blood, broken by Ouessem's wild outbursts of rage, unfold in a slow stretch of time creating a syncopation that transforms splatterfest into zombie opera. The scene stretches on and on until finally he is dispersed into the crowd, disappearing among the hands that are gouging out his entrails.

What happens watching this scene is that this unlikable cop becomes individuated. The violent outburst of energy with which he meets death gives him a face, an identity that sets him apart from all the survivors and the great teeming horde of an undifferentiated zombie mass. He realises the paradox Zygmunt Bauman articulates of being individuated in liquid modernity:

> In a society of individuals everyone *must* be an individual; in this respect, at least, members of such a society are anything but individual, different or unique. ... Paradoxically, 'individuality' is a matter of 'crowd spirit' and a demand enforced by a crowd. To be an individual means to be *like* everyone else in the crowd – indeed identical with everyone else.
>
> *(Bauman, 2005: 16)*

Zombies embody this spirit of crowd spirit. They hunt out difference and devour it. For some years now zombies have been getting quicker on their feet and more directed in their movements. From the humble sensors of blood, sound and movement in *Night of the Living Dead* they have become a mob on the run, wide-awake to a whiff of individuality. Individual survivors in zombie movies commonly ape zombies as a way of surviving, mimicking the zombie shuffle, the moan, even rolling in blood in order to pass unnoticed in a zombie horde. In other words, they're enacting the quandary Bauman puts forward in *Liquid Life*: 'when individuality is a "universal must" and everybody's predicament, the sole act that would make you different and so genuinely individual would be to try – bafflingly, stupefyingly – *not to be* individual' [italics in original] (Bauman, 2005: 16). These frenetically energised moments of fragmented montage, when limbs, entrails and mouths penetrate and fuse in a frenzy of digestion, promise a final arrival at oneness when the disincarnated self is reincarnated in the faceless horde. Here this visual moment of supreme violence forges an encounter between the viewer and the conundrum of individuation in late modernity. It's only in this one moment of supreme violence that the film manages to say something, and again because of its grammar, because it reiterates the formal operatic relationship between the crowd and individuated narrative that Romero learns from Duras as a way of making 'horror rise again from its ashes' (Duras, 1961: 9).

Socialising zombies

But some zombie fictional works are moving in the opposite direction magnifying the socio-political space of individuated narrative while the zombie chorus loses its power of punctuation, of sounding 'time' on the human drama. *The Walking Dead* (2010) is a curious example of this. As the series develops the *absurdity* of zombies as a theatrical premise is falling away. *The Walking Dead* is deadly serious. Three seasons in – and I haven't laughed yet. In the place of hilarity, horror and disgust – *The Walking Dead* is *earnest*. A long-drawn-out exercise in the implications of apocalypse to ordinary American values, it imagines a future of moral dilemmas. As the first two seasons unfold the action shifts from surviving the zombie horde to a moral battle between the two key male characters. Rick and Shaun have been friends since childhood and partners as policemen before the apocalypse. In their former life, the codes of masculine friendship have limited and defined their relations to women. The season opens with them conversing in a shared lament about the difficulties of women, their irrationality, their demands, but the apocalypse intervenes and open competition soon replaces fraternal friendship. Believing Rick dead, Shaun falls in love with Laurie (Rick's wife) but once they are reunited with Rick he starts to reveal his inner zombie. He is the zombie within, the one Freud warns is waiting in the wings for the moment when repression lifts in war and killing/murder becomes approved. Constantly agitating against any decisions made on moral grounds, he urges Rick to assume the sacrificial logic he thinks the situation demands. For Shaun, others are there to help or heed but have no intrinsic value as human beings. The authority of the law rests with the strongest male and, once he is established, the woman is ultimately his to claim.

But good and evil don't present a great challenge to us in *The Walking Dead*. Pressured by Shaun, Rick decides to execute a young man who knows the group's whereabouts and is part of a gang of raiders, but good man Dale intervenes, providing a moving oration on the necessity of sustaining rule by law and the sanctity of life. Dale ends up being 'put down' in a benevolent act following a zombie attack but, in dying, he resanctifies the law, uniting the group around his vision of a moral humanism. The prisoner is freed (only to be killed by Shaun) but Rick never strays again from the path of benevolent and moral leadership advocated by Dale, the lawgiver and symbolic father of the new 'tribe'. Shaun is killed once as a man and once as a zombie, and the group reforms around Rick, who by the third season has become its uncontested leader.

In the third season the group of survivors we have come to know and identify with are locked in battle with another group of survivors – inhabitants of a new township founded by a charismatic leader, 'The Governor'. His utopian township hides a dystopian underbelly. The communal solidarity of the town is held together by the violence of its ceremonies and is defended by a fraternal gang of brothers who, at the command of the Governor, loot and kill, to feed and arm the group. The Governor's charismatic charm moreover hides a killer's pleasures. No social contract defends these people from his whims. They live in the rim of his fantasy, buoyed up by his rhetoric, and his military power, but undefended from the madness of his imaginary – as we discover when we watch him dispatch his militia to kill other survivors and anyone who dares to leave his rule. It's a future society returned to a primitive past providing an elementary lesson in the necessity of violence to form a social contract founded on law rather than might.

The popularity of *The Walking Dead* has to do with the way it charts a path of survival in an apocalyptic future while negotiating the fears that feed anxiety in everyday life in late modernity. Rick and Laurie's marriage falters but love prevails – when Laurie dies. Family groups disassemble and reassemble into unfamiliar *ad hoc* groups that become familiar over time – or don't. The dramatic action unfolds across cityscapes and landscapes awash with the litter of mass consumption, luxuries of the past converted into useless trash. In one of the best of these scenes, Rick rides into Atlanta on horseback wearing his sheriff's uniform and toting a bag of guns, but, as a reverse of the conquering cowboy, when his horse rounds a corner a mass of zombies have him on his hands and knees in a matter of minutes, crawling through the refuse of a wasted city with the mauling dead all around. It's an exacting depiction of the end of a myth: the new frontier is a wasteland of derelict buildings, burnt out army tanks and thousands upon thousands of hungry consumers desperate for a bite of anything left alive. In another memorable sequence, Dale quotes a fragment of Faulkner to the astonishment and wonder of the survivors. In this post-apocalyptic world a fragment of a poem or a song-verse assumes the status of rare treasure salvaged from a 'past' hard at work forgetting its treasury of culture. The survivors continue to search for signs of God's intention in a reality that mocks the idea of a divine plan. As Hershel says in 'Beside the Dying Fire' (2012a), Season 2, Episode 13: 'God promised a resurrection of the dead. I just thought he had something different in mind.' And at every point the survivors are implicated in killing: directly and indirectly they kill zombies en masse, survivors in opposing groups and, when necessary, each other.

But in working through these fears of society gone amok, *The Walking Dead* is creating a new kind of zombie epic in which the intensity of zombie scenarios is deflected into an episodic exploration of the impasses of contemporary culture projected onto an apocalyptic future. Political and social critique is an intrinsic part of the genre but in this series it begins to assume the lead role. The zombies start to become secondary, just part of the working day of the survivor's life-struggles. Normalised and integrated into the landscape they become ordinary. The lure of the characters' story lines, the details of their everyday lives, losses and loves begins to renormalise time as narrative triumphs over the viscid and visual intensities of the zombie chorus. Even the zombie feast loses its symbolic power as the characters who die become more significant than the dead, or than death itself. When Laurie dies, we don't see the moment of her death but the tearful goodbyes endure for an entire sequence. The slaying of zombified erstwhile intimates starts to become routine. The burial of the dead and the renewal of funeral rituals replace rotten corpses. *The Walking Dead* is fast becoming an ongoing lesson in first year Sociology, and as its social commentary rises its allegorical power diminishes. *The Walking Dead* socialises zombies projecting a world where absolute risk is the condition of the working day, but where even on the far side of death it seems law triumphs and sociality holds the moral few in the cup of its hand. As such, despite its manifest social 'content', *The Walking Dead* starts to assume the function of creating a post-apocalyptic *habitus*: a space of future dwelling that — albeit challenging — allows its viewers to imagine life continuing in a zombie world. No longer punctuated by the raw violence of the zombie chorus this social commentary loses its poetic power. Slowly opera is diminishing to the simulated reality of the individuated dramas playing out on the screen. This diminishment of the allegorical power of zombies is a reminder that fiction doesn't gain its power of critique through mirroring social reality but rather through poetic figurations of a social world that is never known or mapped in advance. The power of zombie scenarios to illuminate the relation between individual lives and the abstract social systems that drive them in late modernity can't be realised through 'telling' but emerges out of a mobile poetics in which the self's singular tune begins and ends with the chorus line.

Decomposing zombies

Jay Lee's lewd and ludic *Zombie Strippers* (2008) provides a contrary example in which the extreme violence of the zombie chorus fuels the allegorical power of the text. As funny as it is obscene, this R-rated (18+) film is not for mainstream viewing, despite the fact it sustains a highly conscious interrogation of the necro-politics in play in zombie erotics. Mocking the genre and its viewers, *Zombie Strippers* creates a centrefold of the erotic desires animating zombie fans, a close-up of what it means to chose death over life. In lieu of narrating survival, the film explores the unconscious desire to be zombie. Remaking the absurdist premise of Ionesco's (1960) *Rhinoceros* – in which all but one man forsakes individuality for the pleasures of becoming a rhinoceros – Lee creates an absurd scenario in order to foreground the erotic necrophilia captivating zombie audiences. Inverting the opposition between survivors and the zombie horde, Lee creates a satire which super-heats the allegorical power of the genre even as he is undressing it. *Zombie Strippers* is all chorus, a vortex of gyrating dead bits punctuated by fragments of narrative that never take on the semblance of reality.

Lee's characters lack character; they never stray from type. 'The girls' – strippers at 'Rhinos' – conform to all the clichés of mindless inanity that one might expect to find in a *representation* of women strippers in an R-rated movie. Obsessed with their bodies and their beauty, they live for the tips and the ogling desire of the cretins that come to watch them strip. The club's owner is sleaze incarnate, a money-grubbing, satin-suited obsessional who disinfects the air around him, fears the touch of 'his girls', but fingers the money *sans cesse*. The janitor is an illegal immigrant, a 'Senor illegal' who gets to clean up the blood, brains and all the other unpleasant waste products of the strip-joint while being incessantly abused by the club's owner. The dialogue of these clichéd characters is empty, repetitive and nonsensical. They make as little sense as the world they're inhabiting – a world turning into zombie. In contrast, Lee's zombies disobey all the basic premises of what a zombie can and can't do. They talk, they dance, they have intentions and their emotional baggage carries over into the after-life. In short, they lack the *je ne sais quoi* that defines zombies as the subjectless dead. These zombies hold a grudge against rival strippers, read Nietzsche and perform lap-dances on the face of the boss before eating him.

The film's overt political 'message' has the same quality of ostentatious typicality as its characterisation. As a satirical epistle against the American industrial military complex it has all the sophistication of a newly converted left-wing student circa 1977. Absurdity is unrelenting, culminating in a news report on a corporation working on a chemo-virus designed to ease the shortage of soldiers in a military fighting wars on every front:

> It's a chemo-virus designed to reanimate the dead tissue and jump start the brain. This would allow a soldier say, to continue fighting after death. After one experiences death fear is almost gone. It enhances the combat mind-set.
> (Zombie Strippers, 2008)

Even death has a use-value in war, American style. Predictably the American military let the virus out, the marines are sent in, and one bitten soldier attempting to escape execution (marine-style) flees to the neighbouring strip-club where the real satire unfolds, a hyperbolic montage of death which captivates audiences in the image of themselves erotically captivated by death.

Zombified, Lee's zombie strippers just keep on dancing and as they're disencumbered of their flesh they become more and more irresistible to their slavish male audience. But here the erotic element is explicit, unavoidable and magnified by the utterly stupid dialogue of utterly stupid individuals: 'This is going to be so great. Wow! Your hands are cold. That's interesting!. You're tongue is so dry … I'll get it wet' [as the zombie stripper bites off the man's penis] (*Zombie Strippers*, 2008). Or, on the part of the still-living strippers yearning to be desired like their dead colleagues: 'I'm beautiful … Do you think I'm beautiful? … I'm doing it the whole flesh-eating zombie stripper thing' (*Zombie Strippers*, 2008). Finally a sole couple remains individuated and, in a repetition of Ionesco's sole human in a world of rhinoceri, must decide whether to join the mass or remain human. Ultimately, they talk their way back into being human through language that reassumes the power of meaning. Charged by a marine to prove she's human in a 'deeply ontological way' (*Zombie Strippers*, 2008) Jessie and her boyfriend stumble through a litany of pop-culture references until finally Jessie has a memory:

> I just had a memory. I'm in a field and I look down and I see a single dandelion growing out of what looks like cow-manure and suddenly a wind blows and the wind is aswarm with glistening floriades milk-blue in the afternoon sun and I've never seen such profound beauty rising up from cow-shit.
> (*Zombie Strippers, 2008*)

The violence of the zombie feast finds its limit and its allegorical power here in this movement back into an individuated story – which some might want to dispense with as a jaded moment of a defunct humanism – but in the aftermath of bodies flailing into decomposition this *something* seems a whole lot better than *nothing*.

This isn't just a moment of naive individualism. Jessie's isolated moment of reflexive self-awareness detonates in language, and through language, puncturing the seamless display of visual monstrosity. In becoming human again – in stepping back into meaning – she provides an allegorical springboard. Distinguished at this moment from the horde of spectators who have fed themselves to the pleasures of consuming death, her memory of 'glistening floriades milk-blue in the afternoon sun' (*Zombie Strippers*, 2008) condenses memory itself, and affect, and, moreover, the possibility that one might step back from a cultural industry saturating its viewers with the pleasures of mass-cannibalism. In the midst of a postmodernist pastiche of violent

FIGURE 4.1 Zombie marines, zombie parade, Adelaide, October 2012.

montage, Jessie *gestures* to Ionescu and his *modernist* critique of conformity. It's a dramatic operatic gesture taking in its sweep the problem of the self in a culture of mass zombiism, the possibility of the singular art work sounding within the vast fragmenting genre of horror, and the existential problematic of being an I, that persistent and irreducible embodiment of memories, affects, reflexivity – and death. What's curious about this moment from a sociological point of view, is that 'I' is Jessie's only choice in a world fast becoming zombie, but this 'I' is only recovered when a marine has a gun pointed at her head.

5

CARRION DREAMS

> worn dandies, shaven fools with stinking breath,
> pale varnished corpses, grey decrepit beaux,
> the world-wide rhythm of the Dance of Death
> is sweeping you to shores no mortal knows![1]
>
> — Charles Baudelaire (1931)

Social thinkers have been telling us for over a century that the denial of death is intrinsic to modernity, but zombie fictions head contrariwise into an obscene, explosive and super-heated encounter with death. But they do so with a festive air – dancing at the graveside. *Zombieland* (2009) is a good example. Obsessed with finding the last Twinkies in post-apocalyptic America, the two protagonists, Columbus and Tallahassee, cross the country, taking out zombies as they go. As Columbus says: 'When Tallahassee goes hulk on zombie he sets the standard on not to be fucked with. No fear. Nothing to lose … what can I say, it's like Art' (*Zombieland*, 2009). 'Art' takes the form of Tallahassee attracting a zombie by strumming a banjo then using it to bash its head in, or decapitating a zombie with a pair of garden clippers as Columbus and Tallahassee trade stories of the best and most bizarre zombie kills. Zombie 'kill of the week' is a woman who drops a piano on a zombie, which makes for a laugh as the zombie goes splat! These festivities escalate in a First Nation arts and crafts shop where the survivors play a game of smash, trashing their way through the shop to the sounds of Mozart's *Figaro*. We could interpret this as an allegory for the desecration of culture (both First Nation American and that of western civilisation) but the fun far outweighs any critique. As Columbus says, 'enjoy the little things even if that means destroying a whole lot of little things' (*Zombieland*, 2009). Even girls in fairy dresses, 'fucked up little monsters' (*Zombieland*, 2009), get trashed for a laugh as they are dragged across the asphalt clinging to a bumper bar. The film reaches its festive end at an amusement park where Tallahassee finally gets his share of Twinkie bars, and as a bonus gets to shoot zombies in an every-which-way display of cowboy pizazz until piles of bodies fill the fair ground. Game playing with death is endemic to the genre. In *Dawn of the Dead* (2004) survivors on neighbouring rooftops play post-apocalyptic charades. One side names a celebrity, the other side identifies the zombie look-alike in the zombie crowd by shooting the right zombie in the head. In such scenes killing zombies mutates from an act that the zombie apocalypse necessitates into a promise of post-apocalyptic fun.

Danse macabre

We could understand such works as creating an imaginary habitus for a future where killing is without sanction or, as working to keep death at bay – in the psychoanalytic sense of a negation (death is raised up in order to keep it repressed). But there are powerful cultural precedents for dancing with death even as it clutches and leers. In the aftermath of the crises of the fourteenth century – the Black Death, the papal schism and the Hundred Years War – the *Danse Macabre*'s grim allegories of death dominated the visual and poetic imaginary of medieval Europe. Despite its closed theological referents, the imagery of the *Danse Macabre* has a lot in common with zombies. These medieval skeletons blow trumpets, burst from graves and leak entrails from open bodies as they dance and snatch at the living. Death takes all, with a similar grotesque humour, in the *Danse Macabre*: popes, lords, rich merchants sitting down to a hearty supper, young girls at the height of their beauty, the fresh-faced, the world-weary, the rich and the poor. And then, as now, this all-consuming death incites a festive element – a dance at the graveside. Like the imagery of the zombie apocalypse these skeletal figures warn of a future reckoning while at the same time making a funfair out of death.

Death: 'hidden in the light'

When people dance with death in the world of zombie could they be attempting to foment a new symbolic and imaginary rapport to their own finitude just as the *Danse Macabre* did in the aftermath of the Black Death? This idea goes against the grain of much contemporary critical thinking on how modern subjects encounter death and the role that representation plays in this. Freud argued that in modern society there is a pervasive denial of death. We accept that death is natural, undeniable and inevitable and yet at the same time we attempt in every way to eliminate it from life. When we imagine our own death, Freud argues, we do so only as spectators who survive it. As psychoanalysis reveals, 'in the unconscious every one of us is convinced of his immortality' (Freud, 1918: 11). Commenting on this passage, Samuel Weber (1997) suggests that the implication here is that, when we think about death through the act of representation, we transform death into a spectacle and ourselves into spectators, thus ensuring that we miss the very thing that is at stake – our own finitude. As he writes:

> Imagining death thus becomes the opposite of what it seems: a way of ostensibly overcoming the threat of non-being, of no longer being there, in the world. To 'think' death in this way, as representation, is to idealise it: to transform it into an appearance that preserves that from which it is abstracted.
>
> *(Weber, 1997: 85)*

Many zombie fictional works give credence to this view in their ostentatious celebrations of a death that seems at far remove from the real losses of death of both self and others. Could participants in zombie scenarios be observing a spectacle that enables them to enjoy the feast of death that zombies enact, to be mesmerised by it and in full enjoyment of the murderous pleasure it promises, while remaining untouched by any sense of death itself or its relation to the self?

Despite everything I've said thus far, I'm not convinced of this, at least not as a blanket statement about the relationship between death and representation when it comes to zombies. Zombie scenarios manifest death at every turn; they keep death in our line of vision, spell-bind us with the body opening out its entrails to our gaze, literalise those things we fear most – decay, cadavers, mutilation – and render us constantly in apprehension at the nearness of death. It's true nobody dies. Zombie films and zombie festivals enable their participants to be alive in the face of death, to feast on death, to murder at will (in fantasy), to be dead and yet to live on. Hence all those marchers moaning so joyfully for Braiiiins. But I don't think zombie scenarios in either their filmic or social forms let their participants off the hook quite so readily.

The idea that we engage with literary and other fictional forms, in a non-implicated way – as detached observers – belies the destabilising and cachectic power of fiction and the power of the forms of identification it constitutes. The affective relations established between a text and its readers involves an identification with the lives of others in their complexity, and literature (and other fictional forms) has the capacity to open up a multi-perspectival reality that snares its readers, not in a flat, abstracted or linear line of thought but in all the contrariness of being and non-being. Literary worlds are as much about empty spaces as about presences. When we enter into a fictional work, we live the emptiness – the fall into non-being – of those we identify with. To conceive of this affective landscape as a spectacle for our observation misses the way fictional works have the capacity to provoke emotional and cachectic experience and moreover, to ironise the denial of death itself. Consider Leo Tolstoy's (1981 [1886]) *The Death of Ivan Ilyich* and the encounter it provokes between death and the reader through its representation of Ilyich's slow journey into *the idea* of his death. Ilyich is a character who embodies Freud's denial of death but Tolstoy pursues this denial relentlessly as Ilyich turns and twists away from the mounting evidence of his moribundity. He knows that 'Caius is a man; men are mortal; therefore Caius is mortal' (Tolstoy, 1981 [1886]: 79), but he doesn't inhabit this knowledge until his dying body takes him kicking and screaming to the place where he must encounter himself as Caius. Dreams, pains, anguish and anxiety torment him as his body forces his mind to finally register that he can, and will, fall out of his own sentence. His 'I' is what is at stake in this relentless path towards non-being, and the reader who follows him is not invulnerable to the encounter the novel forges for the reader with the end of his or her own 'I'.

I *know* because I read this book when I was a young woman, and – as it seemed at the time – dying. I didn't observe Ilyich's fate as a detached observer: I lived every shrinking minute with him as he squirmed and resisted the fate in store for him. I was doing the same thing – but Tolstoy's lens enabled me to recognise myself reflexively in Ilyich's great struggle to accept that death was a word that had him in it. Death is hard work – as anyone who comes close to dying knows – but the great storehouse of literary and fictional representations of death are tools of the trade.

Freud's thesis on the denial of death has become something of a verity in contemporary theory and is repeated in the influential writing of thinkers as diverse as Jacques Derrida and Bauman. Echoing Freud, Bauman (2006: 42) writes, 'I can't imagine the world from which I am absent without imagining my own presence in it as witness, camera-man and reporter.' Bauman reiterates that the self can only experience death through the death of others. Viewing the televised deaths of strangers we care little about, he argues, allows us to recognise death as an inevitable reality but only as an abstract statistical notion. The far more shattering death of those we love provides us with a second order of experience, an oblique insight into the meaning of death. Intertwined as our lives are with the lives of others, their loss can give us an experience of death 'once removed'. But Bauman (2006: 44) avows, 'this is the sole modality in which the experience of death is accessible by the living'. At the same time, he argues that death is ever-present metaphorically. In the liquid modern world death 'twice removed' haunts every waking minute in its endless reiterations of sudden loss. Death is the motivating compulsion in the games of *Big Brother* and the *Biggest Loser*, the evictions in these reality TV shows allowing their avid participants to experience death – by proxy. Contemporary sites of breakage and loss, the failures of intimacy, the precariousness of lives lived in a world where jobs, families and partnerships can terminate at any point create a permanent threat of impermanence. Death is 'hidden in the light', everywhere but nowhere, endlessly threatening to capsize the space of life.

The writing of historian Philippe Ariés (1974), sociologist Norbert Elias (1985) and anthropologist Geoffrey Gorer (1977) places a different stress, however, on the denial of death. In lieu of death conceived as an existential impossibility for the human psyche to grasp, they contrast the elision of death in modernity to that of earlier societies in which social rituals and ceremonies sustained a collective rapport to a *proximate* death. Philippe Ariés (1974) traces the gradual transformation of western attitudes to death from a consciously orchestrated and heavily ritualised communal event to an isolated, individuated and unmentionable occurrence. Between Keats' (1819/1999) desire for an easeful death and Tolstoy's awareness of the social stigma of dying, death itself drops from view. Ariés argues that modernity produces a new death, *invisible death*, its horror unmediated any longer by collective ceremonies. The only form of mediation with this new way of dying is through the medical profession who sanitise its filth, banish its emotion and domesticate the nature it speaks. Writing in the 1960s, British anthropologist Geoffrey Gorer (1977) also described the progressive erasure of British mourning rituals and how, in the absence of rituals, the traditional British fear of emotion takes over. In the 1980s Norbert Elias (1985) pleaded for the dying in their loneliness abandoned by collective ritual. Death as a learned social experience, he argued, falls prey in modernity to collective amnesia. No longer speaking its presence in the transience of life, no longer requiring divine intervention to secure permanence, death retreats, and with it communal solace for the dying. The only visible death is the death of the other, not the Romantics' beloved other but another reduced to pure corporeality. Faced with this de-subjectivised death narcissism is able to sustain its myth of immortality. Death appears momentarily to have moved into an untroubled future, pushed back in time by medicine's advance. Elias, Gorer and Ariés lament this passing of death as the death of culture itself: 'Dying is at present a largely unformed situation, a blank area on the social map' (Elias, 1985: 28). Leaving this area blank, they argue, sociality fails at the level of narrative to secure its place within time and hence it can no longer hold time in its tracks. How, they ask, can new rituals be created that will carry the burden of death as death moves closer to us all in the wake of modernity's collapse?

Waste matters

One answer to that question might be 'zombies'. Zombies bring death into the light in its most unrelieved and naked state. Death by zombies knows no limits. The body explodes, its inner secrets exposed to the light, its invisible matter rendered visible. The cadaver walks into our world and holds our vision to its grim portents of our future waste.

For French psychoanalyst Julia Kristeva, there is nothing more threatening to the psyche than the cadaver, a fearful and threatening object that signifies the inevitability of our becoming waste. In confronting the cadaver, she writes, we confront our ultimate incapacity to secure the borders of our being:

> there I am at the border of my condition as a living being. My body extricates itself as being alive from that border ... such wastes drop from me so that I might live, until from loss to loss, nothing remains in me and my entire body falls beyond the limit ... Cadaver.
>
> *(Kristeva, 1980: 3)*

Far from positing an incapacity to apprehend our finitude, Kristeva argues that individuals are permanently under threat from the incomplete nature of the ordered and bound state of the ego. The term Kristeva uses for the traces that recall the ego to its incapacity to be in complete mastery of itself is the *abject* – forms of human waste such as blood, excreta and phlegm that both repel, disgust and fill us with desire. The zombie exemplifies this abject object. As corpse, it is both us and not us, the thing which we fear being and that which we will inevitably become. As a living corpse, a corpse still animated by brute desire, it mirrors our profound fear, bewilderment and fascination with the process of dying – our sentient transition into thing. What is it, she asks, that annihilates all the safeguards we have to defend our boundaries and keep the inside in, and the outside out? Establishing the self involves excluding all that is not the self, spitting and excreting the effluent that is of the body, but not the body. To maintain the bound self we have to extricate ourselves from the claim this waste matter makes on us. But what we thrust aside in order to live eventually becomes us:

> If dung signifies the other side of the border, the place where I am not and which permits me to be, the corpse, the most sickening of wastes, is a border that has encroached upon everything. It is no longer I who expel. I is expelled.
>
> (Kristeva, 1980: 3–4)

Zombies play a strange game with abjection. Like a photographic portrait shot with too short a focal lens, they give us a distorted close-up of ourselves as the waste-self that haunts the psyche. Zombie fictional works constantly play on the self – mutating into zombie. Mirrors play a key role here, capturing and reflecting a zombie self back to survivors struggling to sustain the boundary between themselves and the walking dead. In 'Save the Last One', episode 3 of Season 2 of *The Walking Dead* (2011a), Shaun's reflection takes on a zombie hue as he shaves in a mirror the morning after he has sacrificed Otis, a fellow survivor, to the zombies. His justification for shooting Otis has been altruistic – he needs to get medical supplies back to the other survivors in order to save a young boy's life. Feeding Otis to the zombies is the only way he can buy time for his own escape. But, as the camera moves between Shaun's reflected image and his shaved hair falling into the bathroom basin, the viewer sees the zombie in the mirror, the wasted matter flowing down the drain. Murdering Otis has perforated the boundary separating him from them. *Shaun of the Dead* (2004) makes a game of this doubling of zombies and humans by a clever choreography in which the somnambulistic movements of people waking, walking, shopping and commuting on a normal weekday morning take on the rhythmic automatism of a zombie shuffle. It's a proleptic vision. No one is dead – yet! But they might as well be. In this parody of the anaesthetised state of contemporary mass culture we are all somnambulists drifting into death. More devastatingly, many zombie films create survivor narratives in which men, liberated from social law, zombify as they return to the state of the primal horde. In gestures, reflections, mute actions and blunted affects such men signify the cadaver that lurks within.

But zombies are waste matter that won't fall away, waste matter that returns from the grave to pursue the living to the point of death. They are the *walking-waste*, a mobile metaphor that fuses the existential waste that haunts our psychical lives with the ontological waste that haunts our social lives. And zombies always get in. Walls, doors, gates, locks – those elemental forms of defence that humans rely on to demarcate inside and outside, self and other – fail utterly to create a barrier able to defend the self, or the socius, from the return of this mobile waste. As the genre has evolved, those first planks and nails that failed to defend the farmhouse in *Night of the Living Dead*, have proliferated into every conceivable mode of fortification from armoured tanks, walled townships, high-tech bunkers, shopping malls, to itinerant tent cities. But every fortification erected to keep the walking waste at bay succumbs to a pressure that is both internal and external. Fortifications hold out the promise of a defended psyche – a self, a group – but inevitably all boundaries are porous. The self falls into dissolution.

In *28 Days Later* (2002) the survivors travel across the United Kingdom in response to a radio message that promises a refuge defended by the army only to be entrapped in a fortified castle where the army-unit intends to make use of the useful (the women) and render waste the useless (the non-compliant man). Jimmy finds himself the next victim in a massacre site but the dead are not zombies – they are humans wasted by the army. Zombies are always leading humans to spill out of their built worlds and driving them back into them. In 'Seed', episode 1 of

Season 3 of *The Walking Dead* (2012b) the survivors have become vagrants – driven from the safety of Herschel's farm by a stampeding mob of zombies – and are dwelling in makeshift camps by night and running by day. They eventually find shelter in a former prison with zombies outside the fence, zombies in the neighbouring cellblocks, and former convicts both inside and out. In a zombie future only a prison can offer a transient refuge from being a refugee of the apocalypse. This constant vagrancy mirrors the increasingly itinerant nature of contemporary life where professionals and refugees alike assume lives of ceaseless mobility. But these survivors have none of the caché of today's mobile professionals (Elliott and Urry, 2010); instead, as apocalyptic cast-outs, they conjure up the image of millions of stateless itinerants in search of refuge in the leaking boats, tent cities, detention centres and the new camps of late modernity. Endlessly displaced from one shelter after another, they travel across the country in search of asylum, which, once found, becomes the new fault-line of defence. And, like today's nationalist parties obsessively railing against the incursion of borders long penetrated by globalisation, they build defensive systems against a threat they carry with them. Neither the psyche nor the socius can defend against the delible borders of imagined boundaries. Both boundary-rider and border-crosser, survivors fuse agonistic relations into a shared fate – all are visited. These remnant groups of humans who have lost the shelter of society bespeak our deepest fears of culture falling into waste. They evoke Elias's (1985) lament that, as we moderns lose the capacity to find ways of narrating, ritualising and touching our transience, our finitude, we will lose a place in time itself.

As a mobile figure of waste encircling and encroaching on life, zombies signify a saturation point; a collective need to relearn the exigencies of death. In the globalised mediatised world, death is a tidal wave crashing on every psyche hooked into global networks that ceaselessly represent the world's chaos. In this age of death denial there is no let-up in the spectacle of the death of others dying en masse in wars, tsunamis, from HIV, from famines, from freak storms and freak heatwaves. But the only *médecins sans frontières* to aid the affliction of a death-saturated psyche emerge in fantasy. Zombie scenarios narrativise the loss of time, the moment when past, present and future fuse, and only death is left at work – devouring the space of life. They seed their viewers with the imagery of death and provide a space to endlessly rehearse the loss of the self and all its others. Like those medieval scythe-wielders they pluck their viewers out of the myth of immortality and hurl them into a spectacle of death writ large: of the self, of the family, of society, of the world. They create an imaginary dwelling place in which to envisage the moment when we all become the subjectless dead – the moment when bodies stripped of their individuation merge with the flotsam of the world's waste; when the compulsion to be individuated risks losing the thing that makes us human, our being individuals in and of society. They provide a spectacle of our becoming one with those all subjects consigned to living death. Zombies are fictive manifestations of what Giorgio Agamben (1998) has called bare-life: subjects outside the law and able to be killed with impunity. When they break down the fortifications that defend survivors from rapacious destruction they create a conduit for the imagination to experience what it is to live undefended, by law, by state, by taboo. They bring waste to our door and provide a means within fantasy for us to forge a relation between our death and the death of others, the death that haunts our nightmares and fills our waking hours with its ceaseless spectacle.

So what is a zombie? I'm starting to think that trying to understand zombies is like shuffling a Rubik's cube that has no solution. But, as Jacques Lacan (1992) points out, if we get the answer we're expecting to a question then it's not really an answer. This captures the way zombies keep slipping the net, each answer only gives rise to a new paradox. As we've seen zombies are metaphors that slip across the semantic field gathering and condensing meaning in ever new and more improbable ways. They can be both Democrats and Republicans, they can signify stagnation and mobility, enslavement and insurrection, lethargy and voracity. If we attempt to define their meaning we lose sight of their mobility *as metaphor*. The fact that zombies are no longer textually bound complicates this as does the fact that their textual manifestations are so amorphous and contradictory. I've suggested that zombie is a metaphor that allows us to think about those things we are least able and most need to think about in the early twenty-first century, but I've also looked at some of the worst moments of unthinking in zombie works and by zombie fans. I've suggested that identifying with zombies and participating in their theatrics provides a way of gaining proximity to the pleasures of murder and war, and that part of their fascination has to do with an eroticised fear and fascination with death. I've argued that zombie texts can be the stupidest of works and the most eloquent, that they celebrate violence and critique it. I've suggested that zombies give death a new immediacy, restore it to its rightful centre stage in an age of death denial, and yet at the same time appear to offer a joyful reprieve from death, making a carnival of the death of others. I could keep arguing the toss about what it is zombies do and what we do with zombies when we make meaning with them. But I'm going to give the last word in this book to a dream that puts me in mind of how zombies – for all their faults – are *metaphorai*, they take us on journeys 'to shores no mortal knows' (Baudelaire, 1931).

Carrion dreams

When I was a young woman in my twenties, I fell ill one day walking home from work. It was a hot day steaming with the humidity Sydney brews up in late December. I thought it was the heat, the humidity, the long day at work, but by the time I had made my way across the city bizarre things were happening to my vision and my balance. I was about to embark on a strange journey: a trip to hospital that would last several years and take me again and again to the edge of death. Long before I could apprehend the dire state of things I started to dream. Drifting in and out of sleep I would find myself on a beach watching the surf roll in, wave after wave crashing into the shore. Out at the edge of the breakers, the translucent green lip of each new wave rose up and revealed its carrion load: dead bodies, limbs, torsos; each long doleful roll heavy with the dead of generations. Thousands of them, hundreds of thousands of them – their empty grins flashing up as the waves formed and broke. Wave after wave dumped its load on the shore and then sucked at my ankles, the undertow pulling me back into the sea.

Dreams, as we know from psychoanalysis, are the royal road to where 'it' thinks. In this dream 'it' seems to be taking me to the place where 'I' become 'that' – *in time* – marked by the repetitive suck of the sand around my ankles. After death receded and time opened out again, the dream stayed and became a touchstone to live by. As Freud (1918: 18) says in *Reflections on War and Death*, 'If you wish life, prepare for death.' The ongoing memory of this dream is a *memento mori* sustaining a visceral and visual trace of the shock of death in the life of my *self*, that micro-world of affects, memories, others and narratives that ends with me. It holds in check the idea that death – any death – can be brushed aside. Up close, death clutches at your entrails, fills you with fear, shocks the life right out of you. Just like a zombie film, the dream takes the eye to the cadaver and holds it there, multiplying its horror in countless thousands. It forges a relation between the eye that views and the body that rots. And it forges a spectacle of death that holds me in it; I am *implicated* in what I see. There's no relief in this vision; no narrative deflects the implicit message in the image. There is no theological answer, no meditation capable of returning the eye to a future vision of return. Instead the eye follows the waves from the horizon line into the shore as the undifferentiated dead of ages past roll into the present where my two feet stand sinking into a transient and drifting sand-bed. The unconscious creates such dreams when we can't make sense of the matter at hand; and right now the collective psyche is dreaming – zombies.

NOTES

1 Monstration

1 *Macquarie Dictionary Online* (2013) defines a bogan as: *noun Colloquial (mildly derogatory)* 1. a person, generally from an outer suburb of a city or town and from a lower socio-economic background, viewed as uncultured; originally typified as wearing a flannelette shirt, black jeans and boots, and having a mullet hairstyle … 2. a loudmouthed, stupid person; yobbo.
2 *Macquarie Dictionary Online* (2013): *noun Colloquial* 1. a can of beer … Also, tinny.
3 Bauman uses the term liquid modernity as an alternative to postmodernity. Liquidity implies the emergence of a radical lightness, mobility increased freedoms – and anxiety.
4 In Victoria in 2009 unprecedented heatwaves were followed by the worst bushfire in Australia's recorded history which burnt out 4,500 square kilometres of land and left thousands of people homeless and many hundreds bereaved.
5 See, for instance, Pym (2012) on the way 'zombie companies' are preventing economic growth in Britain.

2 The collective zombie

1 Zora Neale Hurston's (2009) *Tell My Horse*, and Wade Davis's (1988) *Passage of Darkness: The Ethnobiology of the Haitian Zombie* provide compelling ethnographic accounts of zombification. Alfred Métraux (1959) doesn't believe in zombies but his rich ethnographic study *Voodoo in Haiti* is illuminating, as is Joan Dayan's (1998) *Haiti, History and the Gods* for its textual analysis of Haitian literature and culture. Kyle William

Bishop (2010) provides one of the best contemporary analyses of this fractured and over-determined field of scholarship and makes insightful comments about the inherent dangers and abuses in the knowledge-power games in play over what is and isn't a Haitian zombie.

3 Zombie erotics

1 There are exceptions. In Jay Lee's *Zombie Strippers* (2008) Kat is a zombie who reads Nietzsche; in *Land of the Dead* (2005) the zombie Big Daddy is armed with instrumental intelligence, a weapon and empathy for his fellow zombies.

5 Carrion dreams

1 The original French verse is: 'Antinoüs flétris, dandys à face glabre,/ Cadavres vernissés, lovelace chenus,/ Le branle universel de la danse macabre/ Vous entraîne en des lieux qui ne sont pas connus!' Baudelaire (1993 [1857]).

BIBLIOGRAPHY

28 Days Later (2002), motion picture, United Kingdom: Twentieth Century Fox. Dir.: D. Boyle.
28 Weeks Later (2007), motion picture, United Kingdom: Twentieth Century Fox. Dir.: J.C. Fresnadillo.
ABC News (2011) 'Mexico zombie walkers aim at world record', available at <http://abcnews.go.com/Entertainment/slideshow/mexico-zombie-walkers-aim-world-record-15035953> (accessed 10 January 2013).
Ackerman, H.W. and Gauthier, J. (1991) 'The ways and nature of the zombi', *The Journal of American Folklore*, 104:414, 466–94.
Adler, L. (2000) *Maguerite Duras: A Life*, trans. A. Glasheen, Chicago, IL: University of Chicago Press.
Agamben, G. (1998) *Homo Sacer: Sovereign Power and Bare Life*, trans. D. Heller-Roazen, Stanford, CA: Stanford University Press.
Albom, M. (1997) *Tuesdays with Morrie*, New York: Broadway Books.
Ariés, P. (1974) *Western Attitudes to Death: From the Middle Ages to the Present*, trans. P.M. Ranum, Baltimore, MD: John Hopkins University Press.
Aristotle (1996) *Poetics*, trans. M. Heath, Harmondsworth: Penguin Books.
Arnzen, M.A. (1994) 'Who's laughing now? The postmodern splatter film', *Journal of Popular Film and Television*, 21:4, 176–84.
Arsova, I. (2012) '12,000 undead make zombie walk the biggest ever', *I Love Chile* website, available at <http://ilovechile.cl/2012/10/23/zombie-walk-on-the-streets-of-santiago/70490> (accessed 13 January 2013).
Artaud, A. (1938/1970) *The Theatre and its Double: Essays by Antonin Artaud*, trans. V. Corti, London: Calder.

Bibliography

Austen, J. and Grahame-Smith, S. (2009) *Pride and Prejudice and Zombies*, Philadelphia, PA: Quirk Books.

Badiou, A. (2005) *The Century*, trans. A. Toscano, Cambridge: Polity Press.

Bakhtin, M. (1981) *The Dialogic Imagination*, M. Holquist (ed.), trans. C. Emerson and M. Holquist, Austin, TX: University of Texas Press.

Barthes, R. (1980) *Camera Lucida: Reflections on Photography*, trans. R. Howard (1981), New York: Hill and Wang.

Bataille, G. (1986 [1957]) *Erotism, Death and Sensuality*, trans. M. Dalwood, San Francisco, CA: City Lights Books.

Baudelaire, C. (1993 [1857]) 'The danse macabre', in *The Flowers of Evil*, trans. J. McGowan, Oxford: Oxford University Press.

Bauman, Z. (2003) *Liquid Love*, Cambridge: Polity Press.

—— (2004) *Wasted Lives: Modernity and its Outcasts*, Cambridge: Polity Press.

—— (2005) *Liquid Life*, Cambridge: Polity Press.

—— (2006) *Liquid Fear*, Cambridge: Polity Press.

Beck, U. (1992) *Risk Society: Towards a New Modernity*, trans. M. Ritter, London: Sage.

Beck, U. and Beck-Gernsheim, E. (1995) *The Normal Chaos of Love*, trans. M. Ritter and J. Wiebel, Cambridge: Polity Press.

—— (2001) *Individualization: Institutionalized Individualism and its Social and Political Consequences*, trans. P. Camiller, London: Sage Publications.

Behuniak, S.M. (2011) 'The living dead? The construction of people with Alzheimer's disease as zombies', *Ageing and Society*, 31:1, 70–92.

Benjamin, W. (1955) 'Theses on the philosophy of history', *Illuminations*, trans. H. Zohn, Suffolk: Fontana Collins, 1973, 255–66.

Bergen, P. (2011) *The Longest War: The Enduring Conflict Between America and Al-Qaeda*, New York: Free Press.

Bishop, K.W. (2010) *American Zombie Gothic: The Rise and Fall (and Rise) of the Walking Dead in Popular Culture*, Jefferson, NC: McFarland & Company.

Black, M. (1954) 'Metaphor', *Proceedings of the Aristotelian Society*, 55, 273–94.

Blinkley, T. (1974) 'On the truth and probity of metaphor', *Journal of Aesthetics and Art Criticism*, 33:2, 171–80.

Brooks, M. (2003) *The Zombie Survival Guide: Complete Protection from the Undead*, New York: Crown Publications.

—— (2006) *World War Z: An Oral History of the Zombie War*, New York: Three Rivers Press.
Brown, R. (2011) 'Zombie apocalypse? Atlanta says bring it on', *New York Times*. Available at <http://search.proquest.com/docview/898823506> (accessed 6 November 2012).
Callois, R. (2001 [1939]) *Man and the Sacred*, trans. M. Barash, Urbana, IL: University of Illinois Press.
Censky, A. (2012) 'The myth of the zombie economy', *CNN Money*, available at <http://money.cnn.com/2012/07/16/news/economy/zombie-economy/index.htm> (accessed 10 January 2013).
Christie, D. (2011) 'A dead new world: Richard Matheson and the modern zombie', in D. Christie and S.J. Lauro (eds) *Better off Dead: The Evolution of the Zombie as Post-human*, New York: Fordham University Press, pp. 67–80.
Cohen, T. (1976) 'Notes on metaphor', *Journal of Aesthetics and Art Criticism*, 34: 3, 249–59.
Columbus, G. (2012) 'Undead come alive: thousands invade Ashbury for zombie walk', *Ashbury Park Press*, available at <www.app.com/article/20121006/NJNEWS/310060058/Undead-come-alive-Thousands-invade-Asbury-Zombie-Walk?nclick_check=> (accessed 12 January 2013).
Crick, F. and Koch, C. (2001) 'The zombie within', *Nature*, 411: 6840, available at: <www.nature.com/nature/journal/v411/n6840/full/411893a0.html> (accessed 6 November 2012).
D'Alterio, E. (2012) 'Is "zombie building" trend ruining our cities?' *Architecture Source*, available at <http://designbuildsource.com.au/australian-architect-warns-zombie-building-trend> (accessed 17 October 2012).
Davis, W. (1985) *The Serpent and the Rainbow*, New York: Simon and Schuster.
—— (1988) *Passage of Darkness: The Ethnobiology of the Haitian Zombie*, Chapel Hill, CA: University of North Carolina Press.
Dawn of the Dead (1979), motion picture, United States: United Film Distribution Company. Dir.: G. Romero.
Dawn of the Dead (2004), motion picture, United States: Universal Pictures. Dir.: Z. Snyder.
Dayan, J. (1998) *Haiti, History and the Gods*, Berkeley, CA: University of California Press.
de Man, P. (1984) 'The epistemology of metaphor', in M. Shapiro (ed.) *Language and Politics*, New York: New York University Press.

Domm, P. (2012) 'Signs we are approaching a zombie economy', *CNBC*. Available at <http://finance.yahoo.com/news/signs-approaching-zombie-economy-194723167.htm> (accessed 18 October, 2012).

Drezner, D.W. (2011) 'How I learned to stop worrying and love zombies', *The Chronicle of Higher Education*. Available at <http://chronicle.com/article/How-I-Learned-to-Stop-Worrying/126306/> (accessed 17 January 2013).

Duras, M. (1961) *Hiroshima Mon Amour: A Screenplay by Marguerite Duras*, trans. R. Seaver, New York: Grove Press.

The Economist (2010) 'The zombie hypothesis: health-care reform', available at <www.economist.com/node/15453116> (accessed 6 November 2012).

Elias, N. (1985) *The Loneliness of the Dying*, trans. E. Jephcott, Oxford: Basil and Blackwell.

Elliott, A. and Urry, J. (2010) *Mobile Lives*, New York: Routledge.

'Face Off', *Breaking Bad* (2011) television programme, United States: AMC. 9 October.

Ferguson, H. (1995) *Melancholy and the Critique of Modernity: Soren Kierkegaard's Religious Psychology*, London: Routledge.

Friedrich, E. (1987 [1924]) *War Against War*, Seattle, WA: Real Comet Press.

Freud, S. (2001 [1913]) 'Totem and taboo', in J. Strachey (ed. and trans.) *The Standard Edition of the Complete Psychological Works of Sigmund Freud*, Vol. XIII, London: Vintage, pp. 1–162.

—— (1918) *Reflections on War and Death*, e-book, trans. by A.A. Brill and A.B. Kuttner, New York: Moffat, Yard and Company. Available at <www.gutenberg.org/catalog/world/readfile?fk_files=2083540&pageno=1> (accessed 15 January 2013).

Fukada, S. and Nakamura J. (2011) 'Why did "zombie" firms recover in Japan?' *The World Economy*, Asia regional issue, 34: 7, 1124–37.

Gabriel, M. and Žižek, S. (2009) *Mythology, Madness and Laughter: Subjectivity in German Idealism*, London: Continuum.

Game of Thrones (2011) television series, United States: HBO.

Giddens, A. (1992) *The Transformation of Intimacy*. Stanford, CA: Stanford University Press.

Google (2012) 'Google trends: zombie', available at <www.google.com.au/trends/explore#q=zombie&cmpt=q&geo=ID> (accessed 20 November 2012).

Gorer, G. (1977 [1965]) *Death, Grief and Mourning*, New York: Arno Press.

Gordon, A. (1997) *Ghostly Matters: Haunting and the Sociological Imagination*, Minneapolis, MN: University of Minnesota Press.

Grahame-Smith, S. (2009) *Pride and Prejudice and Zombies*. Philadelphia, PA: Quirk Books.

Hiroshima Mon Amour (1959), motion picture, France: Cocinor. Dir.: A. Resnais.

Hurston, Z.N. (2009) *Tell My Horse: Voodoo and Life in Haiti and Jamaica*, New York: Harper Perennial Modern Classics.

In Treatment (2008) television series, United States: HBO.

Ionesco, E. (1960) *Rhinoceros and Other Plays*, trans. D. Prouse, New York: Grove Press.

I Walked with a Zombie (1943) motion picture, United States: RKO Radio Pictures. Dir.: J. Tourneur.

Johnson, M. (ed.) (1981) *Philosophical Perspectives on Metaphor*, Minneapolis, MN: University of Minnesota Press.

Juan of the Dead (2012), motion picture, United States: Outsider Pictures. Dir.: A. Brugués.

Keats, J. (1819/1999) 'Ode to a nightingale', *John Keats: Selected Poems*, London: Penguin Classics.

Kee, C. (2011) '"They are not men ... they are dead bodies!": from cannibal to zombie and back again', in D. Christie and S.J. Lauro (eds) *Better Off Dead: The Evolution of the Zombie as Post-human*, New York: Fordham University Press, pp. 9–23.

Kuchment, A. (2011) 'Zombie insects: a Q&A about a sinister virus', *Scientific American*. Available at <www.scientificamerican.com/article.cfm?id=zombie-insects> (accessed 6 November 2012).

Kundera, M. (1978) *The Book of Laughter and Forgetting*, trans. A. Asher (1996), New York: Harper Collins.

Kristeva, J. (1980) *The Powers of Horror: An Essay on Abjection*, trans. L.S. Roudiez (1982), New York: Columbia University Press.

Lacan, J. (1966) *Écrits: A Selection*, trans. A. Sheridan (1977), London: Tavistock Publications.

—— (1992) The Seminar of Jacques Lacan, Book VII; The Ethics of Psychoanalysis, 1950–1960, ed. J.A. Miller, trans. D. Porter, London: Routledge.

Lakoff, G. and Johnson, M. (1980) *Metaphors We Live By*, Chicago, IL: The University of Chicago Press.

La Horde (2010), motion picture, France: Le Pacte. Dir.: Y. Dahan and B. Rocher.

Land of the Dead (2005), motion picture, United States: Universal Pictures. Dir.: G. Romero.

Matheson, R. (2004 [1954]) *I am Legend*, London: Gollancz.
Métraux, A. (1959) *Voodoo in Haiti*, trans. H. Charteris, New York: Oxford University Press.
Murch, B., Espinosa, D. and Andell, H. (2012) 'The indy eye: zombie march 2012', *The Argentina Independent*, available at <www.argentinaindependent.com/multimedia/photoessay-multimedia/the-indy-eye-zombie-march-2012/> (accessed 12 January 2013).
Nature (2012) 'Zombie star rising', *Nature*, 482: 443. Available at <www.nature.com/nature/journal/v482/n7386/full/482443b.html> (Abstract only accessed 6 November 2012).
New Oxford Dictionary of English (1998) Oxford: Oxford University Press.
Night of the Living Dead (1968) motion picture, United States: Walter Reade Organization. Dir.: G. Romero.
Piaget Shanks, L. (1931) *Flowers of Evil*, New York: Ives Washburn.
Poulet, G. (1969) 'Phenomenology of reading', *New Literary History*, 1:1, 53–68.
Pym, H. (2012) '"Zombie" companies eating away at economic growth', *BBC News: Business*, available at <www.bbc.co.uk/news/business-20262282> (accessed 15 January 2013).
Quiggin, J. (2011) 'Why zombie ideas persist in economics', *The Chronicle of Higher Education* 57: 29, available at <http://chronicle.com/article/Why-Zombie-Ideas-Persist-in/126754/> (accessed 6 November 2012).
Ratliff, E. (2005) 'The zombie hunters', *The New Yorker*, 81:31, available at <www.newyorker.com/archive/2005/10/10/051010fa_fact> (accessed 6 November 2012).
Redneck Zombies (1989) VHS, United States: Trans World Entertainment. Dir.: P. Lewnes.
Richards, I.A. (1936) *The Philosophy of Rhetoric*, Oxford: Oxford University Press.
Ricoeur, P. (1978) *The Rule of Metaphor: Multidisciplinary Studies in the Creation of Meaning*, London: Routledge and Kegan Paul.
Rozen, D.E. (2011) 'Parasites and zombie gammarids', *The Journal of Experimental Biology*, available at <http://jeb.biologists.org/content/214/19/iv.full> (accessed 6 November 2012).
Rutherford, J. (ed.) (1997) 'Diana: the hour of our death', in Ien Ang (ed.) *Planet Diana: Cultural Studies and Global Mourning*, Kingswood, NSW: University of Western Sydney Press.
Scott, R. (2008) '"Now I'm feeling zombified": playing the zombie online', in S. McIntosh and M. Leverette (eds) *Zombie Culture:*

Autopsies of the Living Dead, Lanham, MD: Scarecrow Press, pp. 169–184.

Seabrook, W.B. (1989 [1929]) *The Magic Island*, New York: Paragon House.

Shaun of the Dead (2004) motion picture, United Kingdom: United International Pictures. Dir.: E. Wright.

Shaviro, S. (1993) *The Cinematic Body*, Minneapolis, MN: University of Minnesota Press.

Smith, K.M. (2010) 'Lansetkòd: memory, mimicry, masculinity', in L. Gordon (photography and oral history) *Kanaval: Vodou, Politics and Revolution on the Streets of Haiti*, London: Soul Jazz Records, pp. 71–106.

Sontag, S. (2003) *Regarding the Pain of Others*, New York: Farrar, Straus & Giroux.

Spolar, C. and Sebert, L. (2012) '"Zombie buildings": are they the next economic calamity?' *Huffington Post Investigative Fund*, available at <www.huffington post.com/2009/11/20/zombie-buildings-are-they_n_365400.html> (accessed 17 October 2012).

Spring, T. (2005) 'Spam slayer: slaying spam spewing zombie PCs', *PC World*, June 20 2005, available at <www.pcworld.com/article/121381/article.html>.

Stanley, D. (2012) 'The nurse's role in the prevention of Solanum infection: dealing with a zombie epidemic,' *Journal of Clinical Nursing*, 21:11–12, 1606–13.

Stanley, T.L. (2010) 'Toyota Corolla touted as anti-zombie shield', *Brandweek*, 51:40, 21.

Steiner, G. (2001) *Grammars of Creation*, London: Faber & Faber.

Sydney Zombie Walk (2013) *Press Information*, available at <www.sydneyzombiewalk.com/press> (accessed 13 January 2013).

Terkel, S. (1984) *The Good War: An Oral History of World War II*, New York: New Press.

Tolstoy, L. (1981 [1886]) *The Death of Ivan Ilyich*, trans. L. Solotaroff, New York: Bantam Classics.

The Undead Report (2012) 'Hone your apocalypse skills with zombie shooting this fall', available at <www.undeadreport.com/2012/09/hone-your-apocalypse-skills-with-zombie-shooting-this-fall/> (accessed 10 November 2012).

Urban Dictionary (2013) 'Urban Dictionary LLC', San Francisco, available at <www.urbandictionary.com/define.php?term=zombie> (accessed 10 January 2013).

The Walking Dead (2010), television series, 2010–2012, United States: AMC.

—— (2011a) 'Save the Last One', Season 2, United States: AMC. 30 October.
—— (2011b) 'Secrets', Season 2, United States: AMC. 20 November.
—— (2012a) 'Beside the Dying Fire', Season 2, United States: AMC. 18 March.
—— (2012b) 'Seed', Season 3, United States: AMC. 14 October.
Waller, G.A. (1986) *The Living and the Undead*, Urbana, IL: University of Illinois Press.
Warner, M. (2006) *Phantasmagoria*, Oxford: Oxford University Press.
Weber, S. (1997) 'Wartime', in H. de Vries and S. Weber (eds) *Violence, Identity and Self Determination,* Stanford, CA: Stanford University Press.
White Zombie (1932), motion picture, United States: United Artists. Dir.: V. Halperin.
Yakir, D. (1977) 'Morning becomes Romero', *Film Comment*, 15: 3, 60–65.
Žižek, S. (1992) *Looking Awry: An Introduction to Lacan through Popular Culture*, Cambridge, MA: MIT Press.
Zombie (1932) Written by Kenneth Webb. Performed New York, Biltmore Theatre. Performance: Theatre.
Zombie (2011) *Brisbane Zombie Walk*, available at <www.brisbane zombie walk.com/welcome/> (accessed 15 January 2013).
Zombie Apocalypse (2010), DVD, United States: Eagle One Media Distributor. Dir.: R. Thompson.
Zombieland (2009), motion picture, United States: Columbia Pictures. Dir.: R. Fleischer.
Zombie Strippers (2008), motion picture, United States: Stage 6 Films. Dir.: J. Lee.
Zombie Wars (2008), DVD, Germany: EuroVideo. Dir.: D.A. Prior.
Zomblies (2010), motion picture, United Kingdom: Realm Pictures. Dir.: D.M. Reynolds.

INDEX

28 Days Later 4, 38, 93
28 Weeks Later 6

abjection 91–2
Ackerman, Hans W. 31
Adelaide, Australia 1–2, 29
Agamben, Giorgio 95
aggression 42–4
ambivalence 6, 41–2, 44–5, 52, 56, 66
apocalyptic futures 3, 14, 44, 76, 94
Ariés, Philippe 90
Aristotle 19
Austen, Jane 3, 12–13

Badiou, Alain 26–7
Bakhtin, Mikhail 11–13
Barthes, Roland 50–1, 53
Bataille, George 53, 55–9
Baudelaire, Charles 84
Bauman, Zygmunt 4, 8, 35–6, 74–5, 89
Beck, Ulrich 5–8, 13, 21
Benjamin, Walter 9
Bishop, Kyle William 31
borders 91–2, 94
Breaking Bad 11
Brook, Max 13

Callois, Roget 46
carnival 29, 30, 37, 50

catastrophes 8–9, 95
children 6, 49; in zombie parades 3, 53–4, 59–60
colonialism 35–7, 67

danse macabre 85–6
Davis, Wade 29, 33–4
Dawn of the Dead 38, 85
death and photography 50–1, 53; *see also* photography
death denial 84–90, 94–6
dreams 97–8
Drezner, Daniel 21
Duras, Marguerite 68–73, 75

Elias, Norbert 90, 94
emotions, uncomplicated, of zombies 41–2, 52
eroticisation of death 10, 55–9, 62, 80–1

family, destroyed by zombies 5–6, 66, 77
films 2–5, 7, 10–11, 35–8, 44, 61–75, 79–85, 93; and social/political critique 10, 67, 72–3, 75, 81
Freud, Sigmund 39–45, 76, 86, 88–9, 97
Friedrich, Ernst 69–70

Game of Thrones 11
Gauthier, Jeanine 31
genres, zombies infiltrating 12–14, 16
Gorer, Geoffrey 90
graffiti 1–2
Grahame-Smith, Seth 12–13
guilt 45–6

Haiti 29–34, 36–7
Hiroshima 68–9, 71
Hiroshima Mon Amour 68–73
hope, end of 8–9
Horde, La 73–4
Hurston, Zora Neale 32–3

I am Legend 64
identification 39–40
individualisation 5–8, 56, 68, 72, 74–5, 82–3
industrialisation 38, 63
In Treatment 11
I Walked with a Zombie 38

jouissance 63
Juan of the Dead 10

Kanaval 29–30, 37; *see also* carnival, Haiti
Kristeva, Julia 91–2
Kundera, Milan 27

Lacan, Jacques 10, 15, 37, 95
Land of the Dead 38
lawlessness 7, 14, 44, 46, 66, 76–7, 95
left-wing politics 1, 27, 29, 81
Lee, Jay 79–80
literature 3, 12–13, 64, 87–8
Locke, John 19–20
love 5–7, 44, 66, 72; destroyed by zombies 4–7, 42, 77

masculinity 7, 44, 55, 76
Matheson, Richard 64–5

metaphor 19–24, 59, 93, 95–6
metatrope 24
Métraux, Alfred 35
Milat, Ivan 46
modernity 7–9, 12–13, 35–6, 63–4, 74–5, 77, 84, 89–90
murder 44–7, 52, 54–5

Night of the Living Dead 2, 10, 15, 36–7, 61, 65–8, 72–3, 75, 93
novelisation 11–13

photography 48–51, 53–4, 59–60
pleasure 29, 39, 45–6, 50, 63, 82, 87, 96
political demonstrations 26–8
pornography 10, 79–81; *see also* eroticisation of death
Poulet, Georges 40
Pride and Prejudice and Zombies 12–13

Redneck Zombies 62
Resnais, Alain 68, 70–3
revolution 1, 10, 28–31, 34–5, 37–9, 64
Ricoeur, Paul 20
risk 8–9, 13
Romero, George 2, 10, 35–6, 38, 61–2, 64–8, 72–3, 75

sacrifice, human 57–8
Sade, Marquis de 53, 55
Scott, Ron 41
Seabrook, William 34–5
sexual violence 7, 38, 54, 55–6, 58, 59–60
Shaviro, Steven 63
slave revolution 30–1, 34, 37; *see also* Haiti
slavery 30–2, 34–9, 67
slogans 1, 29
Smith, Katherine 34
social bonds 4–7, 13, 29, 43–6, 77, 79

Sontag, Susan 69–70
Steiner, George 8–9

taboo 43, 46, 52, 56
television 11, 13–15, 76–9, 92, 94; reality television 89; and social/political critique 78–9, 94
Terkel, Stud 13
Tolstoy, Leo 88
Totem and Taboo 45
Towarnicki, Frédérick de 71
transgression 29, 34, 46, 56–8

vampires 2, 64
video games 41
Voodou 31–2, 34, 35

Walking Dead, The 13–15, 45, 76–9, 92, 94
Waller, Gregory A. 64

Warner, Marina 15–16
war 8, 13, 42–4, 46, 69–70, 73, 81
waste 91–3, 95
Weber, Samuel 86–7
White Zombie 38
World War I 42–3, 69
World War II 13, 69, 70
World War Z 13

Žižek, Slavoj 15
Zombie Apocalypse 38
'zombie economy' 20–21
Zombieland 84–5
zombie parades 2–3, 25–9, 39, 40–1, 46, 48–50, 53–4, 60
Zombie Strippers 10, 79–83
Zombie Wars 37–8
zombies: definitions 15–18, 21–22; as a metaphor 19–24, 39, 59, 93, 95–6
Zomblies 62